Digital Media, Political Polarization and Challenges to Democracy

This book assesses the interplay between social media, political polarization, and civic engagement, focusing on countries with differing media environments, cultural specifics, and degrees of democratization.

Taken from a variety of disciplinary perspectives and based on innovative theoretical interventions and empirically grounded research, the contributions to this volume share a common aspiration to understand the democratic character of the new, and thus far largely unknown, media regime. Such a regime has the potential to both enhance and undermine democracy, in a time where the vulnerability of democracy is more obvious than ever before.

Featuring research from the USA, Western Europe, the Middle East, and East Asia, this book will be of interest to those studying recent political events in these regions, as well as to those scholars of media studies whose research focuses on the inter-relation of politics, communication and the media. This book was originally published as a special issue of *Information, Communication & Society*.

Maren Beaufort is a scientist in the Institute for Comparative Media and Communication Studies at the Austrian Academy of Sciences and the Alpen-Adria-University, Austria. Her research interests include social media, political participation, media effects, media quality, and media literacy. She participates in the European Commission's 'Media Pluralism Monitor'.

Digital Media, Political Polarization and Challenges to Democracy

Edited by
Maren Beaufort

Routledge
Taylor & Francis Group
LONDON AND NEW YORK

First published 2020
by Routledge
2 Park Square, Milton Park, Abingdon, Oxon, OX14 4RN

and by Routledge
52 Vanderbilt Avenue, New York, NY 10017

Routledge is an imprint of the Taylor & Francis Group, an informa business

British Library Cataloguing in Publication Data
A catalogue record for this book is available from the British Library

ISBN13: 978-0-367-19889-3

Typeset in Minion
by Newgen Publishing UK

Publisher's Note
The publisher accepts responsibility for any inconsistencies that may have arisen during the conversion of this book from journal articles to book chapters, namely the inclusion of journal terminology.

Disclaimer
Every effort has been made to contact copyright holders for their permission to reprint material in this book. The publishers would be grateful to hear from any copyright holder who is not here acknowledged and will undertake to rectify any errors or omissions in future editions of this book.

Contents

Citation Information

The chapters in this book were originally published in the journal *Information, Communication & Society*, volume 21, issue 7 (July 2018). When citing this material, please use the original page numbering for each article, as follows:

Introduction

Digital media, political polarization and challenges to democracy
Maren Beaufort
Information, Communication & Society, volume 21, issue 7 (July 2018)
pp. 915–920

Chapter 1

Parametrizing Brexit: mapping Twitter political space to parliamentary constituencies
Marco Bastos and Dan Mercea
Information, Communication & Society, volume 21, issue 7 (July 2018)
pp. 921–939

Chapter 2

Facebook news and (de)polarization: reinforcing spirals in the 2016 US election
Michael A. Beam, Myiah J. Hutchens and Jay D. Hmielowski
Information, Communication & Society, volume 21, issue 7 (July 2018)
pp. 940–958

Chapter 3

Do not blame it on the algorithm: an empirical assessment of multiple recommender systems and their impact on content diversity
Judith Möller, Damian Trilling, Natali Helberger and Bram van Es
Information, Communication & Society, volume 21, issue 7 (July 2018)
pp. 959–977

Chapter 4

Women politicians are more engaging: male versus female politicians' ability to generate users' engagement on social media during an election campaign
Moran Yarchi and Tal Samuel-Azran
Information, Communication & Society, volume 21, issue 7 (July 2018) pp. 978–995

Chapter 5

Commitment in the cloud? Social media participation in the sunflower movement
Yuan Hsiao and Yunkang Yang
Information, Communication & Society, volume 21, issue 7 (July 2018) pp. 996–1013

Chapter 6

Counter-surveillance and alternative new media in Turkey
Bora Ataman and Barış Çoban
Information, Communication & Society, volume 21, issue 7 (July 2018) pp. 1014–1029

Notes on Contributors

Bora Ataman is an Associate Professor of Communication Sciences at Arts & Sciences Faculty at Doğuş University, Turkey. He is currently studying topics such as activist citizen journalism, media activism and counter-surveillance, and journalism safety.

Marco Bastos is a Lecturer in Media and Communication in the Department of Sociology at City, University of London, UK, and an affiliate of Duke University's Network Analysis Center, USA. His work addresses sociological aspects of digital media with a substantive interest in the cross-effects between online and offline social networks.

Michael A. Beam is an Assistant Professor in the School of Communication Studies at Kent State University, USA. His research interests include political communication and new communication technologies.

Maren Beaufort is a scientist in the Institute for Comparative Media and Communication Studies at the Austrian Academy of Sciences and the Alpen-Adria-University, Austria. Her research interests include social media, political participation, media effects, media quality, and media literacy. She participates in the European Commission's 'Media Pluralism Monitor'.

Barış Çoban is Professor of Communication Sciences at Doğuş University, Turkey. His research interests are alternative media, new social movements, and surveillance studies.

Natali Helberger is Professor in Information Law at the Institute for Information Law at the University of Amsterdam, the Netherlands. She specialises in the regulation of converging information and communications markets.

Jay D. Hmielowski is an Assistant Professor in the Edward R. Murrow College of Communication at Washington State University, USA. His research interests include political communication and environmental communication.

Yuan Hsiao is a PhD Candidate in Sociology and a Master's Student in Statistics at the University of Washington, USA. His areas of specialization are quantitative methods, social media, collective action, social networks, and social psychology.

Myiah J. Hutchens is an Assistant Professor in the Department of Public Relations at the University of Florida, USA. Her research interests include political communication and political discussion.

Dan Mercea is Senior Lecturer in the Department of Sociology at City, University of London, UK. He is Associate Editor of *Information, Communication & Society*. He does research in Political Sociology, Social Movements, and Political Communication.

Judith Möller is an Assistant Professor at the Amsterdam School of Communication Research, the Netherlands. In her research she focuses on the effects of political communication, in particular social media and digital media.

Tal Samuel-Azran is the Head of the international Program at the Sammy Ofer School of Communications at the Interdisciplinary Center (IDC) Herzliya, Israel. His main fields of research are political communication, new media, public diplomacy, and media globalization.

Damian Trilling is an Assistant Professor in the Department of Communication Science and is affiliated with the Amsterdam School of Communication Research at the University of Amsterdam, the Netherlands. He is intrigued by the question of how citizens nowadays are informed about current affairs and events in their society.

Bram van Es works in the Research Group for Scientific Computing at the National Research Institute for Mathematics and Computer Science, the Netherlands. He has extensive experience in data analysis and machine learning.

Yunkang Yang is a PhD Candidate in the Department of Communication at the University of Washington, USA. His research areas include political communication, information and communication technology, and journalism.

Moran Yarchi is a Senior Lecturer at the Sammy Ofer School of Communications, and the Head of the Public Diplomacy program, at the Interdisciplinary Center (IDC) Herzliya, Israel. Her main area of research is political communication, especially the media's coverage of conflicts and public diplomacy.

Introduction – Digital media, political polarization and challenges to democracy

Maren Beaufort

> Today democracy is under attack and there are many points in which it is weak and vulnerable to those attacks. In almost every democracy citizens are losing confidence and trust in parties and in governments. There are declines in news audiences and press readership. In Europe only half of the citizens born after 1980 think that it is essential to live in a democracy.

It was with these reflections that W. Lance Bennett (University of Washington) opened his public lecture 'Who Are the People' (Bennett, 2017a), which was broadcast by the Austrian Broadcasting Corporation (ORF) as part of an international symposium on 'Digital Media, Political Polarization, and Challenges to Democracy' hosted by the Austrian Academy of Sciences and the University of York.

The same symposium also gave rise to this special issue of 'Information, Communication and Society', which consists of six selected articles based on papers presented at the conference. Held at the Austrian Academy of Sciences in Vienna from 21 to 22 September 2017 the symposium brought together social scientists from 20 countries and four continents to address the complex interplay between democracy, political participation, political polarization, and the new media environment or as Michael X. Delli Carpini (Walter H. Annenberg Dean at the Annenberg School for Communication, University of Pennsylvania) has termed it, the new 'media regime'. In his keynote speech, Delli Carpini argued that, from a historical perspective, distinct 'media regimes' emerge over time, on the back of economic, political, cultural, and technological changes, and that each regime is associated with different notions of free speech, a free press, democratic citizenship, civic engagement, and the responsibility to participate in the political process. The problem is that we are familiar with the rules and norms of the previously dominant broadcast-based regime, we cannot know with any certainty what is most beneficial or most problematic about the emerging new regime (Williams & Delli Carpini, 2011). While the conference itself had a much broader focus, encompassing a range of topics from theoretical reflection on the changing dynamics of democratic processes and political communication to empirical studies on the radicalization of public debates and campaigns, nationalism, (right-wing) populism, and hate speech, the present special issue focuses on the interplay between social media, political polarization, and civic engagement. It also considers what needs to be done to ensure the democratic character of the new, and thus far largely unknown media regime and explores its potential to enhance and undermine democracy.

The conference was marked by a unifying, invigorating, and captivating sense of a new departure, underlined by a mutual feeling of social responsibility. In this spirit, the various theoretical reflections and empirical studies presented at the conference ultimately revolved around the highly topical and urgent question, 'What is to be done?' However fragmentary any answer to this question must be, as W. Lance Bennett noted, it will on the one hand have to set out from the fact that political polarization cannot be grasped in isolation from its entanglement with neoliberal interests; on the other, it will have to address the overarching question, 'Who are the people?' i.e., the question of democratic sovereignty (Bennett, 2017b) . This question calls for far more than a simple examination of populism as today's allegedly central political problem. As Bennett affirms, 'It's rather a question that gets to the actual survival of democracy itself' (Bennett, 2017a). Against this backdrop, the conference saw discussions of a range of approaches based primarily on analyses of the dynamic interplay between changing conceptions of democracy, changing forms of political participation, and changing media usage behaviour. There is a clear evidence of a transition toward a more participatory, commons-based understanding of citizenship, particularly among young people, a transition that serves to shift the focus from ensuring system performance (via voting and party membership) to supporting the system as such. This transition needs to be understood in relation to the ways in which digitally mediated communication influences – and perhaps organizes – our personal relationship to society and public life (Bennett & Segerberg, 2012). Political actors and researchers therefore have to confront the challenge of how to manage this contemporary shift from established structures of representative democracy – with their group-based identities and mainstream issues – toward a wider repertoire of personalized political experience and individual motivated concerns within a digitally networked society marked by an increasingly participatory understanding of democracy (Seethaler & Beaufort, 2017).

The present issue aims to reflect the various multidisciplinary perspectives that shaped the conference discussions. It contains both innovative theoretical interventions and empirically grounded research that addresses the interplay between social media, political polarization, and civic engagement in very different countries with varying degrees of democratization, diverse media environments, and different cultural specificities. Both the three Western and three non-Western contributions to the issue share a common aspiration to understand the (anti-) democratic potential of the new media environment.

The issue opens with a much-discussed topic in current social debates. In their proof of concept study, 'Parametrizing Brexit: Mapping Twitter Political Space to Parliamentary Constituencies', Marco Bastos and Dan Mercea aim to validate the use of social media signals as a means of modelling the ideological coordinates of the Brexit debate. They find that their model explains 41% of the variance in the referendum vote and show that the referendum outcome can primarily be explained by outrage at material inequality and a nationalistic shift. The authors conclude with a discussion of the conceptual and methodological challenges involved in signal processing social media data to measure public opinion. As they see it, the strength of their approach lies not so much in its capacity to generate predictions, but in the possibilities, it offers for the exploration of ongoing developments, which would otherwise require the extensive, continuous, and expensive use of traditional survey methodologies. While this first article focuses on the methodological possibilities of the ongoing analysis of social media content in the social science, the authors of the following two contributions focus on this content itself. They consider the extent to which the rise of social media as a dominant force in news distribution has led to the stronger isolation of different outlooks through filter bubbles from algorithmic filtering and echo chambers that arise in information environments dominated by like-minded people, as well as assessing the consequences of such developments.

In 'Facebook News and (De)Polarization: Reinforcing Spirals in the 2016 US Election', Michael Beam, Myiah Hutchens, and Jay Hmielowski offer a theoretical and empirical framework for the relationship between social media usage, partisan news exposure, and attitude formation (including affective polarization, depolarization, and homeostasis), by revealing a depolarization process that obeys a model of reinforcing spirals. In order to move beyond correlational relationships, they use 3-wave panel data from the 2016 US Presidential campaign, to show that Facebook message use is related to a moderate over-time depolarization spiral and that people who use Facebook for news are likely to be confronted with both pro-attitudinal and counter-attitudinal messages. They find no evidence of a partisan reinforcing spiral that would lead to increased affective polarization. On the basis of previous research that found that people are more likely to engage in counter-attitudinal exposure and information processing when they receive personalized social and algorithmic recommendations (Messing & Westwood, 2014), the authors contend that the depolarization effects they observed are primarily driven by users encountering counter-attitudinal news, especially incidentally, on Facebook. The study therefore indicates that Facebook news may not be responsible for rising citizen polarization. Furthermore, the findings debunk the theoretical links between social and algorithmic news recommendations on social media. This is also the starting point for the following study, which considers the extent to which the algorithms used to generate news recommendations allow for content diversity. In 'Do Not Blame It on the Algorithm: An Empirical Assessment of Multiple Recommender Systems and their Impact on Content Diversity', Damian Trilling, Judith Möller, Natali Helberger and Bram van Es examine the effect of multiple recommender systems on different diversity dimensions and find that all of the recommendation logics in question generate a rather diverse set of recommendations that are on a par with those made by human editors. They also show that basing recommendations on user histories can substantially increase topic diversity within a recommendation set. On the one hand, then, the results of both studies speak against the idea that different political outlooks have become more strongly isolated from one another due to filter bubbles and echo chambers. On the other hand, they point to very specific filtering and acquisitional patterns in use among social networks, which fundamentally differ from those in traditional media environments. These differences should not be underestimated in terms of their impact on engagement and mobilization and require further research.

They can also be seen in the fact that online social networks are regarded as more supportive environments for women than traditional media environments, where previous research has shown that male politicians receive greater coverage (Bystrom, Robertson, & Banwart, 2001; Joiner et al., 2016). The extent to which these newer environments can also help to challenge long-held notions concerning the media inferiority of female politicians is considered by Moran Yarchi and Tal Samuel-Azran in their 'Women Politicians Are More Engaging: Male Versus Female Politicians' Ability to Generate User

Engagement on Social Media During an Election Campaign'. Yarchi and Samuel-Azran examine whether social media offer a more equal platform for female politicians to generate user engagement and mobilize their supporters than traditional media. Taking the 2015 Israeli election campaign as a case study, the authors examine female and male politicians' social media posts with respect to their content and the number of 'likes' and 'shares' they received. They conclude that social media offer greater opportunities for female politicians to promote themselves and raise their status in the political powerplay. While this study focuses on the potential of social media in political public relations and voters' mobilization, the next contribution addresses their role in facilitating bottom-up social engagement.

Do different social media usage types correspond to different forms and levels of engagement and mobilization? In their 'Commitment in the Cloud? Social Media Participation in the [Taiwanese] Sunflower Movement', Yuan Hsiao and Yunkang Yang investigate this question in relation to the commitment of social media participants in digitally enabled protests. They find that the commitment of so-called 'cloud activists' (who operate exclusively online during a movement) is at least on par with most offline participants with respect to their identification with the movement and their efficacy within it. This finding contradicts the traditional notion that only offline participation involves a high level of commitment and suggests that commitment can be exhibited in online forms through sustained or highly intensive organizing activities that may enable (offline) movements to persist. The activities of 'cloud activists' go far beyond those of mere clicktivists (i.e., those who engage in online peer production) and such activists might be regarded as 'virtual connective leaders'. Their use of social media is negatively associated with offline participation, indicating a non-linear relationship between social media usage and offline participation. In contrast to previous studies, the authors find that social media usage serves to increase offline participation only among low and medium level social media users. In general, the authors show that the virtual space consists of different types of actors, whose interrelated usage patterns are non-linear with respect to different forms and levels of engagement and mobilization.

The forms taken by such usage patterns in digital social movements in authoritarian states and the ways in which they contribute to or even enable pro-democracy activism are addressed in the issue's final contribution, entitled 'Counter-Surveillance and Alternative New Media in Turkey'. Here, Bora Ataman and Baris Coban discuss opposing conceptions of surveillance culture and offensive and defensive counter-surveillance tactics in the context of an alternative new media landscape. Ataman and Coban describe how this alternative, independent, critical, and investigative new media landscape has developed away from the traditional mainstream media environment and has come to form a kind of counter-surveillance 'institution'. They make clear that it is only through social media networks – due to their structural characteristics (low access threshold, speed of dissemination, temporal, and local flexibility) and their philosophy (involving anonymity and the possibility of avoiding and changing identifying features, free from formal constraints) – that such a form of counter-surveillance can arise and be maintained. The authors ascribe activists a key role in exposing undemocratic activities. The usage patterns they describe reflect the various actor types elaborated in the previous contribution, along with their interrelations with respect to online and offline activities. In addition, they indicate the particular security demands that have to be taken into account where digital footprints are concerned (Sambrook, 2016) when gathering, producing, and disseminating news (that is considered illegal) in the public debate.

Editing this special issue and collaborating on it with so many committed people has been a pleasure and a privilege.

This collection developed out of the aforementioned Vienna 2017 symposium, which was organized by Brian D. Loader (Department of Sociology, University of York), Josef Seethaler, and myself (Institute for Comparative Media and Communication Studies, Austrian Academy of Sciences and the University of Klagenfurt). Nevertheless, the articles in this special issue do not simply represent the proceedings of the 2017 conference. All of the papers were revised and passed through a double-blind peer-review process and multiple rounds of revisions. I am now delighted to present these six exceptional studies.

I would therefore like to express my deepest gratitude to all the contributors to this special issue for their thought-provoking and insightful contributions. I would also like to thank the anonymous reviewers who, despite the short turn-around time, offered generous and constructive feedback to the authors. I am very happy that this collection is appearing as a special issue of 'Information, Communication and Society'. Many thanks to Sarah Shrive Morrison and Brian D. Loader from the University of York, and Josef Seethaler from the Austrian Academy of Sciences for their valuable help during the editing process. I am especially indebted to W. Lance Bennett for our inspiring discussions during the conference – and that they will continue. Last but not least I owe particular thanks to Marlene Gsenger and Valentina Dopona from the local organizing committee, the Kapsch AG for generously funding the conference, and the Austrian Broadcasting Corporation for the pleasant cooperation.

Disclosure statement

No potential conflict of interest was reported by the author.

Notes on contributor

Maren Beaufort is a junior scientist at the Institute for Comparative Media and Communication Studies (CMC) at the Austrian Academy of Sciences and the Alpen-Adria-University Klagenfurt. Her research interests include social media, political participation, media effects, and media literacy. She participates in the European Commission's 'Media Pluralism Monitor'. Her PhD thesis is concerned with 'media performance and democracy'[email: maren.beaufort@oeaw.ac.at].

References

Bennett, W. L. (2017a). Public lecture "Who are the people". DialogForum at the Austrian broadcasting corporation ORF, 21 September 2017, Vienna, Austria. Retrieved from http://zukunft.orf.at/showcontent.php?sid=147&pvi_id=1820&pvi_medientyp=v&oti_tag=Dialogforum.

Bennett, W. L. (2017b). Who are the people? *Texte: Öffentlich-Rechtliche Qualität Im Diskurs*, *20*, 24–35. Retrieved from http://zukunft.orf.at/show_content.php?sid=147&pvi_id=1815&pvi_medientyp=t&oti_tag=Texte

Bennett, W. L., & Segerberg, A. (2012). The logic of connective action: Digital media and the personalization of contentious politics. *Information, Communication & Society*, *15*(5), 739–768.

Bystrom, D. G., Robertson, T. A., & Banwart, M. C. (2001). Framing the fight: An analysis of media coverage of female and male candidates in primary races for governor and US senate in 2000. *American Behavioral Scientist*, *44*(12), 1999–2013.

Joiner, R., Cuprinskaite, J., Dapkeviciute, L., Johnson, H., Gavin, J., & Brosnan, M. (2016). Gender differences in response to Facebook status updates from same and opposite gender friends. *Computers in Human Behavior, 58*, 407–412.

Messing, S., & Westwood, S. J. (2014). Selective exposure in the age of social media: Endorsements trump partisan source affiliation when selecting news online. *Communication Research, 41*(8), 1042–1063.

Sambrook, R. (2016). Reporting in uncivil societies and why it matters. In S. Cottle, R. Sambrook, & N. Mosdell (Eds.), *Reporting dangerously* (pp. 17–35). London: Palgrave Macmillan.

Seethaler, J., & Beaufort, M. (2017). Community media and broadcast journalism in Austria: Legal and funding provisions as indicators for the perception of the media's societal roles. *The Radio Journal: International Studies. In Broadcast & Audio Media, 15*, 173–194.

Williams, B. A., & Delli Carpini, M. (2011). *After broadcast news. Media regimes, democracy, and the new information environment.* Cambridge: Cambridge University Press.

1 Parametrizing Brexit

Mapping Twitter political space to parliamentary constituencies

Marco Bastos and Dan Mercea

ABSTRACT

In this paper, a proof of concept study is performed to validate the use of social media signal to model the ideological coordinates underpinning the Brexit debate. We rely on geographically enriched Twitter data and a purpose-built, deep learning algorithm to map the political value space of users tweeting the referendum onto Parliamentary Constituencies. We find a significant incidence of nationalist sentiments and economic views expressed on Twitter, which persist throughout the campaign and are only offset in the last days when a globalist upsurge brings the British Twittersphere closer to a divide between nationalist and globalist standpoints. Upon combining demographic variables with the classifier scores, we find that the model explains 41% of the variance in the referendum vote, an indication that not only material inequality, but also ideological readjustments have contributed to the outcome of the referendum. We conclude with a discussion of conceptual and methodological challenges in signal-processing social media data as a source for the measurement of public opinion.

Introduction

The referendum on Britain's membership of the European Union was the flashpoint of more than four decades of Eurosceptic politics contesting the country's membership of the supranational organization (Becker, Fetzer, & Novy, 2016). The vote saw those efforts come to fruition as the British electorate was marginally in favour of leaving the EU, thus opening a new chapter in the political life of the country (Asthana, Quinn, & Mason, 2016) which then embarked on a long process of defining a different relationship with the EU. In this paper, we seek to probe this epochal transformation in British political life by testing whether social media can offer a reliable signal for identifying political alignments as expressed on Twitter. To that end, we provide a proof-of-concept geo-locational analysis of political expression by the British citizenry on Twitter.

Instead of approaching social media analytics as opinion polls, with disputed levels of reliability (Jungherr, Jürgens, & Schoen, 2012; Tumasjan, Sprenger, Sandner, & Welpe, 2011), we examined Twitter data as legitimate manifestations of public opinion in the early twenty-first century (Anstead & O'Loughlin, 2015), similarly to scholarship investigating the public discourse in pre-industrial bourgeois society of the eighteenth century that resorted to, and explored extensively, the circulation of information in discursive arenas such as Britain's coffee houses, France's salons, and *Tischgesellschaften* in Germany (Habermas, 1991). As such, the rationale for this study departs from endeavours seeking to forecast the results of the EU referendum using social media data as a predictor of voter turnout and party affiliation (Celli, Stepanov, Poesio, & Riccardi, 2016).

In view of the alleged political realignment among Western electorates, we probed into the proposition that not solely material inequality, but also ideological readjustments have contributed to the political outcome of the UK voting to leave the EU. From this perspective, outrage at material inequality has been compounded by a reactionary cultural backlash that has been leveraged and maximized by populist parties and leaders (Inglehart & Norris, 2016). To test this proposition, we devised a conceptual model and a coding scheme to classify content along four ideological coordinates and subsequently trained a dedicated opinion-mining parametric algorithm. We rely on this classifier to analyse a large set of Twitter data collected during the referendum campaign.

Twitter content was collected from a range of hashtags and keywords, including Leave and Remain campaign terms such as #takecontrol and #strongerin and terms that provided a forum for deliberating the referendum (i.e., 'Brexit' and 'referendum'). Twitter API was also queried to identify the location of users tweeting the referendum. The data we analyse in the following sections thus includes both ideological and geographic markers. We calculated the ideological leaning of users and subsequently mapped them onto voting constituencies in England, Wales, Scotland, and Northern Ireland. As such, the unity of analysis is not tweets or users, but Parliamentary Constituencies from which we model the prevailing ideological landscape as articulated on Twitter in the run-up to the referendum.

In summary, the deep learning algorithm devised for this study is optimized for identifying ideological affiliation, to pinpoint users' views along a political value space mapped onto Parliamentary Constituencies, and to determine the fit between political expression on Twitter in the period leading up to the vote and the referendum result. In what follows we introduce the conceptual framework underpinning this analysis by unpacking the latent value space before demonstrating its potential for modelling the ideological coordinates of the Brexit debate.

Previous work

Scholarship informing this study stems from two bodies of literature. Firstly, recent surveys suggest that the British population perceive social media as an important complement to their vote, but they continue to occupy a lower position in the wider ranking of news sources covering elections (Dutton, Reisdorf, Dubois, & Blank, 2017). The sense that social media are nonetheless reshaping the media landscape with consequences for democratic politics flows from the argument that either through a conscious choice or algorithmic filtering, users are narrowly exposed to information that reinforces their political outlook (Sunstein, 2007). Such selective exposure entrenches ideological polarization and forecloses reasoned deliberation (Dahlgren, 2009). While evidence-based treatments of this topic have revealed that exposure to a plurality of political views is likely on social media (Bakshy, Messing, & Adamic, 2015; Fletcher & Nielsen, 2017), social dissemination of political content remains more likely among ideologically similar sources (Barberá, Jost, Nagler, Tucker, & Bonneau, 2015).

Secondly, our research was informed by suggestions of a geographical and socio-demographic patterning of voting preferences in the referendum reported in the UK press (BBC, 2016) and scrutinized by academics (Hanretty, 2017; Rennie Short, 2016). The geography of the vote, it was proposed, reflected a socio-economic imbalance between an affluent metropolitan elite clustered in and around London who voted to remain and parts of England and Wales that were economically worse off and voted to leave; secondly, a political cleavage between the seat of the UK government at Westminster, an increasingly independent-minded Scotland, and Northern Ireland whose economic prosperity and political stability have turned on the existence of an open border with fellow EU member, the Republic of Ireland (Rennie Short, 2016).

This study examines public opinion on Twitter against this backdrop of ongoing shifts in deeply engrained ideological leanings (Kriesi & Frey, 2008), which reportedly came to a head in the course of the Referendum campaign (Inglehart & Norris, 2016). We sought to explore whether political talk on social media can quantifiably mirror this process. Specifically, we sought to examine the relationship between communication on social media and the electoral geography of the Brexit referendum to assess the extent to which users tweeting nationalist and populist content would overlap across geographic and cultural zones, and conversely, whether such pattern could be observed in relation to users tweeting globalist or economist content. In other words, we probed whether Twitter public stream can be used to identify, measure, and model the political consequences of an alignment between the vote and broader ideological orientations expressed by the British public opinion.

Following this line of inquiry, the political geography of the plebiscite was unpicked at the level of local authority areas (Becker et al., 2016). By performing a best subset selection procedure, Becker et al. (2016) identified a collection of factors that correlated with the referendum outcome. While contending that a larger turnout in urban areas could have tipped the vote in the other direction, the authors highlighted that the vote to leave correlated positively with a vote for the Eurosceptic UK Independent Party (UKIP) and the British National Party in the 2014 European Parliament elections. Other important correlates of the vote leave were employment in the manufacturing sector, a comparatively lower hourly pay or a higher unemployment rate, the share of rented council housing in the area, longer waiting times for access to the public health system, and lower levels of employment in the public sector.

Demographically, a vote to leave rather than to stay in the EU correlated with the absence of educational qualifications and being 60 years of age or older (Becker et al., 2016). Cumulatively and in accordance with the economic insecurity hypothesis, the socio-economic variables were modelled by Inglehart and Norris (2016) in their analysis of the rise of populism in Europe. This supposition—the economic insecurity hypothesis —pertains to a marked decline in the fortunes of the blue-collar working class faced with contracting real incomes, narrowing access to public services such as health, education, housing, or social welfare in advanced post-industrial economies. Their hardship has been attributed to a political inability to spread the economic benefits of an increasingly integrated global economy (Piketty, 2014).

The authors juxtaposed the prevailing economic insecurity hypothesis to the thesis of a cultural backlash against progressive value change (Inglehart & Norris, 2016). Their hypothesis is that socio-economic hardship and resistance to cultural change are mutually reinforced. The result is a cleavage between, on the one hand, the young and well-educated who embraced progressive post-materialist values foregrounding gender, sexual and racial equality, human rights, environmental protection, secularism, and a greater tolerance of migrants. The other side of the divide is occupied by older, less-educated sections of the population who experienced a decline in their material conditions, along with the perception of gradual erosion of values associated with industrial societies and solidarity around socio-economic positions, religion, race, and geographic location. This section of the UK population saw the cultural politics of identity recognition as a threat to traditional values. Immigration further compounded the disaffection while the EU embodied a cultural threat posed by other European societies, which was felt most acutely among people on the lowest education and income levels, manual workers, and the unemployed (McLaren, 2002).

Socio-economic and cultural realignment of British politics

The scholarship reviewed above foregrounds the thesis that not only material inequality led to the result of the referendum, but also a cultural backlash by older, traditional, and less-educated voters. This open value competition has augmented political polarization within parties based around cultural issues and social identities (Inglehart & Norris, 2016), a development that maximizes political cleavages and deepens the wedge separating culturally divisive issues. The Conservative Party, in particular, has embraced this cultural cleavage by incorporating a nationalist rhetoric in response to European integration and immigration, devolution, rising secularism, and receding influence in world politics (Kriesi & Frey, 2008).

Political realignment is therefore a process that has been in train for some time, albeit masked by the UK's majoritarian electoral system which kept in place the alternation in government between the two large parties (Dunleavy & Margetts, 2001). The electorate has broadly been divided along two cognitive dimensions: an economic and a cultural one (Kriesi & Frey, 2008). The former was dominant for more than two decades from the 1970s to the early 1990s. The latter became increasingly prominent in the late 1990s and early 2000s. If on the economy voters were divided between supporting or reforming the welfare state, on the cultural dimension they were split between the espousal of, on the one hand, liberal political values, environmental protection, and support for European integration and, on the other, traditional values, 'law and order', and a concern with immigration (Kriesi & Frey, 2008, p. 197).

Kriesi and Frey (2008) also showed that Labour and Conservatives converged on a liberal outlook on the economy up to the 1990s, a point of departure when Labour voters became culturally more liberal while Conservatives embraced traditional conservative values. During this period, Labour consolidated its foothold among the highly educated and the middle classes, whereas the Conservative Party attracted the least educated and the working classes through a combination of nationalism and cultural conservativism (Kriesi & Frey, 2008), a process heightened by the emergence of populist parties such as UKIP championing traditional values alongside 'nationalistic and xenophobia appeals, rejecting outsiders and upholding old-fashioned gender roles' (Inglehart & Norris, 2016, p. 30).

Coordinates of the Brexit ideological value space

The conceptual model comprises two axes opposing globalism to nationalism and economism to populism. There are three notable definitions of populism that have guided social science research (Mudde & Rovira Kaltwasser, 2012). Firstly, populism amounts to a movement galvanized by a hypnotic leader that crosses class boundaries; it is, secondly, a manner of doing politics that mainlines the relationship between political leaders and the electorate to the detriment of political parties. Thirdly, populism is a political discourse premised on the claim of greater authenticity in the representation of the experiences and beliefs of an oppressed majority, who sits in antagonism with a hegemonic minority (Laclau, 2005). These definitions have been thrown into question as political parties started to adopt a catch-all response to the erosion of their relationship with the electoral base (Kriesi & Frey, 2008), a process that conflated populism with demagoguery but also took it to the centre stage of party politics.

Despite these developments limiting the analytical value of the concept to the point of being employed as a floating signifier, the three definitions of populism pivot on the variance between 'the people' and 'the establishment' (Mudde & Rovira Kaltwasser, 2012). Asserting socio-economic, political, and cultural alienation, populist discourse further expresses this antagonism as geographical distance separating, for instance, loci of political and economic power such as Brussels, London, or the South-East of England from the rest of the UK (Wills, 2015). The latter embodied a privileged and rootless cosmopolitan elite (Bauman, 2012)—corporate or governmental—vilified as panderers to economic and political globalization personified by the EU and European integration (Kriesi et al., 2008; Woods, 2009).

Nationalist parties have channelled this disenchantment by capitalizing the scepticism of economic trade agreements, technological disruption, and the belief in a culturally and ethnically monolithic state. This homogeneous territory would, firstly, reassert its authority in the face of a perceived abdication of economic self-interest in trade liberalization agreements and, secondly, exert social control over labour migration flows that placed crippling pressure on the institutions of the welfare state (Mudde, 2000, 2004). Conversely, globalism, the third coordinate of the latent ideological space, pertains to a rights-based universalistic worldview that regards individual citizens as free agents operating in a global economy of increasingly convergent national political systems (Turner, 2002).

To summarize, in its more basic forms, populist messages advance a discontent directed at elites and the establishment and foreground popular will, while nationalist sentiments revolve around notions of national exceptionalism, sovereignty, and nativism (Parker, 2016). In opposition to that, a prevalent response to popular disenchantment has been a drive towards greater efficiency in economic policy and analysis, policy-making, and government administration. This is the fourth coordinate in the latent ideological space which we term economism, conceived in opposition to populism and that emphasizes consensus building, due process of law, and accountability, but also expert analysis and evidence-based policy-making that could drive consensus across ideological fault-lines (Nilsson & Carlsson, 2014). As such, economism refers to the comprehensive political consensus to safeguard free market economics embodied in government policy and the array of expert bodies—from the Bank of England to think-tanks, business, and trade organizations—which have helped define and uphold it in the last three decades (Crouch, 1997). Figure 1 shows the ideological coordinates and the political value space that serves as the analytical baseline for this study.

It is against this backdrop of political realignment that the use of social media and data analytics was portrayed as having facilitated accurate canvassing by, for example, the anti-establishment Vote Leave campaign (Cummings, 2016). Equally, social media data have been used to model the result of the vote on June 23rd, based on agreement with the Leave or Remain campaigns expressed on Twitter (Celli et al., 2016). Accordingly, we sought to model the political debate on Twitter in the weeks leading up to the vote and subsequently mapped the value space onto Parliamentary Constituencies (BBC, 2016; Becker et al., 2016; Hanretty, 2017; Rennie Short, 2016). We tested the hypothesis that an economist and globalist discourse would cluster around affluent metropolitan areas with a higher-than-average concentration of groups who have reaped the economic, political, and social benefits of globalization. We concurrently test the hypothesis that economically fragile northern Britain would more readily embrace nationalist, anti-immigration, and populist claims which amalgamate protectionist calls for Britain to shield itself from the global economy, to control flows of people, and to regain its national sovereignty from the EU.

More specifically, we test the hypothesis that the distribution of users advocating either side of the campaign mirrors the results of the referendum (H1). Further, we anticipate the latent ideological space underpinning the classifier maps onto the referendum results across Parliamentary Constituencies, namely along the Globalism–Nationalism polarity

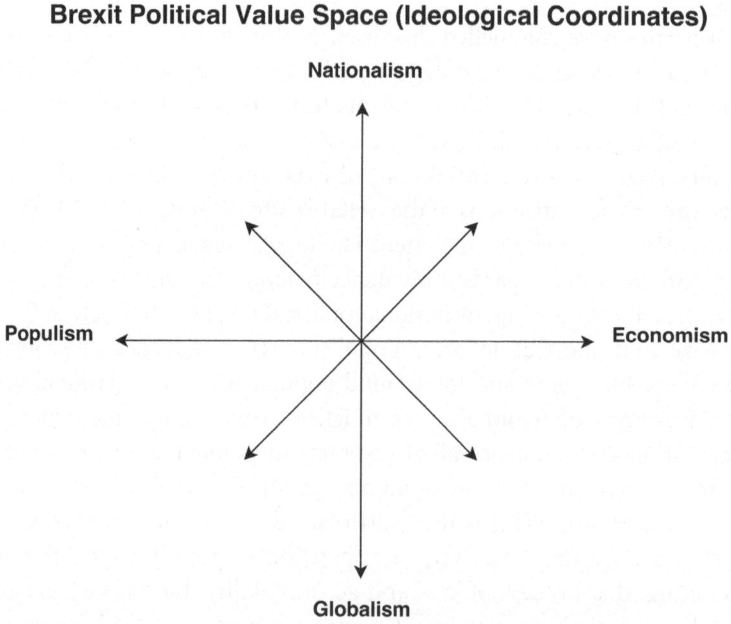

Figure 1. Ideological coordinates of British public opinion and political value space.

(H2), and the Economism–Populism axis (H3). In close relation, we conclude our analysis by modelling the dependent variable RemainPcnt (H4)—the percentage of vote of the Remain campaign—with a multiple regression model that incorporates the abovementioned independent variables (RemainLeave, GlobNat, and EconPop) along with demographic variables retrieved from publicly accessible census data similarly mapped onto Parliamentary Constituencies (ONS, 2011). In sum, the four central hypotheses tested in this study are the following:

H1. The distribution of tweets advocating either side of the campaign matches the vote results across Parliamentary Constituencies (hashtags)
H2. The distribution of Nationalist and Globalist tweets matches the vote results across Parliamentary Constituencies (classifier)
H3. The distribution of Populist and Economist tweets matches the vote results across Parliamentary Constituencies (classifier)
H4. Tweets mapped onto the ideological value space, combined with demographic variables, can account for geographic heterogeneity in the referendum results (multiple regression model).

Data and methods

For the purposes of this study, we relied on the Twitter Streaming and REST APIs to collect a total of 8,821,116 tweets using a set of keywords and hashtags, including relatively neutral tags such as Brexit, referendum, inorout, and euref, but also messages that used hashtags clearly aligned with the Leave campaign: voteleave, leaveeu, takecontrol, no2eu, betteroffout, voteout, britainout, beleave, iwantout, and loveeuropeleaveeu; and hashtags clearly aligned with the Remain campaign: strongerin, leadnotleave, votein, voteremain, moreincommon, yes2eu, yestoeu, betteroffin, ukineu, and lovenotleave. Vocal hashtags supporting the campaigns are leveraged to identify messages advocating each side of the referendum: The Vote Leave or Vote Remain campaigns. We subsequently removed messages tweeted before 15 April 2016, the starting date of the official campaign period, and 24 June 2016, the end of the referendum campaign. Messages flagged as likely to have been tweeted by bots were also removed (Bastos & Mercea, 2017).

Next, we queried the Twitter REST API to retrieve the profile of users that tweeted the referendum. We managed to retrieve 95% of the user profiles that appeared in the data (794,949 out of 834,878). Profile information, along with information tweeted by the users, was pivotal to identifying the location of the user base. We triangulated information from geocoded tweets (subsequently reverse-geocoded), locations identified in their user profile (then geocoded), and information that appeared in their tweets. The triangulation prioritizes the signal with higher precision; hence, geocoded information is preferred if present. When not available, we look at the location field in users' profiles and geocode that location. If neither source of information is available, we check for information in their tweets, but only in cases where the *place_id* field of the API response returns relevant information.

As a result, a considerable portion of user locations in our dataset could be identified only to city or postcode level. Nonetheless, we succeeded at identifying the geographic location of 60% of users that tweeted the referendum (482,193 out of 794,949) who form our population of interest. From this cohort of 482,193 users tweeting the referendum, only 30,122 were based in the UK. Upon identifying the location of users, we removed user accounts located outside the United Kingdom or whose location we could not identify up to the postcode level. This reduces our dataset to 565,028 messages or 11% of all collected messages; a sample of messages that is sufficiently large to allow for testing the hypotheses underpinning this study.

Campaign advocacy

For each tweet, we count the number of hashtags advocating the Leave and Remain campaigns. We tag the message as Remainer or Leaver based on the highest number of vocal hashtags used in association with each side of the campaign. Messages without hashtags advocating either side are tagged as Neutral. The frequency count is aggregated and used to calculate the affiliation of users that tweeted or retweeted hashtags advocating either side of the campaign. Highly polarized messages—i.e., tweets including several supporting hashtags—are however uncommon. For users championing the Vote Leave campaign, only 16% of their messages included more than one such hashtags. These messages are yet more uncommon in the vote Remain campaign, where only 2% of messages included more than one hashtag clearly associated with that side of the campaign.

We conclude the identification of users campaigning for either campaign by calculating the mode or 'mean campaign affiliation' of users based on the frequency of campaign-supportive hashtags used throughout the period. The mean affiliation of users can only be calculated for accounts that actively participated in the referendum campaign on Twitter. In other words, only users that actively tweeted or retweeted content clearly aligned with one side of the campaign are identified in this step of the data processing. We believe this approach, grounded on the mean affiliation per user, reflects strong campaign membership with a low probability of false-positives and below we detail how this measure compares with the variable returned by the machine learning algorithm.

Brexit classifier

The Brexit Classifier is a machine learning algorithm that resulted from multiple tests to identify the four key ideological coordinates explored in this study. We relied on two expert coders who classified 10,000 tweets along the ideological coordinates of Globalism, Economism, Nationalism, and Populism. We controlled for intercoder reliability by double-coding a random sample of tweets ($N = 100$) repeatedly, and after four rounds we achieved a Krippendorff's alpha of 0.94 for the complete value space, with alpha of 1 for the Globalism–Nationalism dyad and 0.86 for the Economism–Populism polarity. We relied on this trained set of tweets to parametrize the machine learning algorithm using text vectorization (Selivanov, 2016), an approach purposefully built for text analysis.

Unlike frequency-based approaches to text classification, which simply compute the number of positive and negative words (or hashtags) and draw a conclusion based on the final sum, text vectorization is a deep learning algorithm that draws context from phrases. It is often deployed to analyse and classify large text corpora, including user feedback, reviews, and comments. The algorithm can handle linguistic variation and performs well with misspelled or poorly constructed sentences, a marker of Twitter communication, because it considers the entire body text of tweets to infer ideological inclination. It is independent from hashtags, though in the Brexit corpus we found hashtagged tweets to be more vocal and likely to display a clear alignment with one of the four ideological coordinates. As a result, and unsurprisingly, the algorithm consistently identifies campaign hashtags as valid indicators of tweets ideologically leaning towards a given position in the political value space.

Training a machine learning algorithm is fundamentally a trade-off between recall (the number of correct results divided by the number of possible results) and precision (the ratio of positive and relevant matches). In other words, the more variables the algorithm has to identify (in our case, there are four: globalism, economism, populism, and nationalism), the higher the likelihood that the algorithm will be unsuccessful. For the purposes of this study, the algorithm needs to identify at least one and a maximum of two ideological coordinates, as the polarities globalism–nationalism and economism–populism are mutually exclusive. Given the disjoint assumption of the political value space, we maximized precision and recall by splitting the ideological value space along two polarities and training two separate algorithms later combined into a single classifier (i.e., the Brexit Classifier). This approach successfully returned substantially more relevant results while also returning most of the relevant results.

We relied on the abovementioned set of 10,000 manually coded tweets to assign a value (positive or negative) to each of the concepts we have sought to map, with the algorithm calculating the probability of positiveness and negativeness for each ideological polarity (Globalism vs. Nationalism and Economism vs. Populism). For each ideological pair, the classifier returns a range of values from 0 (completely globalist) to 1 (completely nationalist), so that values from 0.45 to 0.55 are somewhere in the middle of this scale and assumed to be relatively neutral. The algorithm was trained using Document-Term Matrix (DTM), vocabulary-based vectorization, and the TF-IDF method for text preprocessing. Figure 2 shows the area under the curve on train and test datasets for the

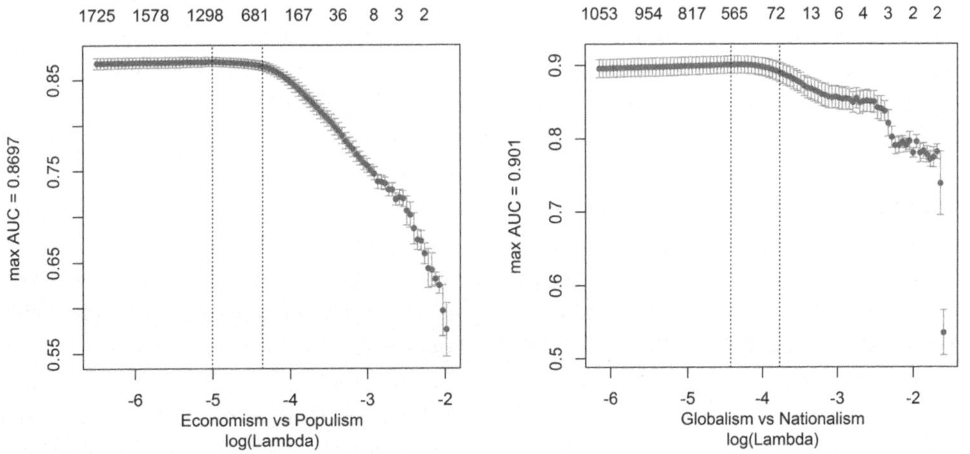

Figure 2. Area under the curve calculated from train and test datasets for the Economism–Populism and Globalism–Nationalism ideological pairs.

Economism–Populism and Globalism–Nationalism ideological pairs (AUC = 0.8697 and AUC = 0.901, respectively). The algorithm performed well for the set of 565,028 tweets explored in this study and we expect it to perform reasonably well in other national contexts in which nativist and populist sentiments might be emerging. In the last step of the classification, the algorithm calculates the best fit, projects the results along spatial coordinates comprising the four ideological dimensions, and estimate significant oscillations between any of the ideological pairs.

Unit of analysis: council wards and parliamentary constituencies

To leverage the granularity of our data, we rely on previous research that successfully mapped the United Kingdom's referendum on membership of the European Union—restricted to local authority level—to parliamentary constituency level using a scaled Poisson regression model that incorporates demographic information from lower level geographies. This approach relies on a principled method of areal interpolation to aggregate the results at the ward or constituency level, along with voting estimates at the level of council wards for authorities that have not disclosed the results at such granular levels (Hanretty, 2017; Huyen Do, Thomas-Agnan, & Vanhems, 2015). The processed referendum data are thus relatively granular with data down to the ward level in England, Scotland, and Wales. As the ward system does not exist in Northern Ireland, the data were aggregated at the Local Authority District, thus overcoming inconsistencies between local authorities and successfully mapping postcodes to Parliamentary Constituencies. In short, we adopt ward-level data when available and estimates of the referendum results where ward-level data were not made available by the authorities. Such estimates advanced by previous research (Hanretty, 2017) allow us to investigate the extent to which the geographic distribution of tweets supporting each side of the campaign and voicing opinions attached to the ideological coordinates mapped in this study interact with the how constituencies voted in the referendum.

Mapping twitter data to council wards and parliamentary constituencies

Mapping geographically rich social media data onto census area or electoral districts is challenging due to the hierarchical subdivision of UK local government areas into various sub-authority areas and lower levels such as enumeration districts. As council wards comprise the most granular level to which we could retrieve results or estimates for the referendum vote, we sought to map referendum-related Twitter activity to this unit of geographic analysis. Therefore, we geocode and reverse-geocode the location of users that tweeted the referendum and subsequently match postcodes to wards and Parliamentary Constituencies using the database provided by National Statistics Postcode Lookup (ONS Geography, 2011). Twitter users are thus simultaneously matched to the fields OSLAUA, OSWARD, and the PCON11CD (Local Authority, Ward, and Constituency codes, respectively). The first field includes Local Authority District (LAD), Unitary Authority (UA), Metropolitan District (MD), London Borough (LB), Council Area (CA), and District Council Area (DCA). Where the council ward system does not exist (i.e., Northern Ireland), data were aggregated using these authorities to cover the entirety of the United Kingdom.

Upon geocoding the self-reported location of users, we found that only 30% of them were based in the UK, with 19% of users that participated in the Brexit debate based in the US and nearly 30% in other EU countries. Also surprising is the large geographic spread of the British Twitter user base, with London accounting for 14%, Lancashire 7%, Kent, Essex, West Yorkshire, and West Midlands ranging 3–4%, and South Yorkshire, Hertfordshire, Cheshire, Merseyside, Surrey, and Hampshire at 2% each. Taken together, each of these geographic groups are of comparable size to London in the share of users that tweeted the referendum.

We ultimately consolidate referendum and Twitter data based on OSLAUA (Local Authorities) and PCON11CD, which is the standardized ID code for each Parliamentary Constituency, the only GSS (Government Statistical Service) beyond European electoral region that is available for Northern Ireland and is consistent across the four countries included in the United Kingdom (ONS Geography, 2017). Using postcode as the common geographic marker across databases, this last step of data aggregation allows for pairing Twitter and referendum data based on Local Authority District, each comprising a range of postcodes. We assigned pseudo codes when no postcodes or grid reference were made available by the authorities, particularly in the cases of the Channel Islands and Isle of Man. Data provided by the Office of National Statistics assigns the range E06 (UA), E07 (LAD), E08 (MD), and E09 (LB) to England; W06 (UA) to Wales; S12 (CA) to Scotland, and N09 (DCA) to Northern Ireland, with the pseudocodes L99 being assigned to Channel Islands and M99 to Isle of Man. Following these procedures, we first calculate the user-average score returned by the Brexit Classifier (Globalism, Economism, Nationalism, and Populism) and the mean campaign affiliation based on advocacy hashtags tweeted by users.

In summary, we calculate the mean campaign affiliation, mean globalist–nationalist, and mean economism–populism for each user that tweeted the referendum. Lastly, we match users to Local Authority Districts to test the hypotheses driving this study. Twitter data are therefore aggregated first at the user level, and subsequently at constituency level, which is the unit of analysis employed in this study. The resulting dataset includes multiple streams of Twitter data consolidated into a single database of online and off-line activity at the constituency level: firstly, their ideological expression on Twitter, and secondly, their voting preferences relative to the 2016 UK EU membership referendum.

Limitations of the methods and data

There are important limitations associated with the ideological polarities developed for this study. Firstly, during the process of training the classifier, we struggled to separate economism from populism, as many of the populist claims are economic in nature. This is reflected in the lower AUC score for Economism–Populism compared with Globalism–Nationalism. We addressed this challenge by accentuating the policy and expert-oriented component of the economism polarity, which sits in opposition to populist views that appeal to emotion and the perceived rights 'of the people', a value that is difficult to unpack but that stands visibly against the value space occupied by economism. Secondly, the clear identification of messages with nationalistic content has limited heuristic value, as nationalistic sentiments in Scotland and England refer to fundamentally different political agendas. Lastly, the various sampling techniques applied to the data, particularly the geographic rendering of user locations up to postcode level, reduced the universe of collected tweet to 11% of the dataset. We expect this set of data to offer a defensible representation of the Brexit debate and our conclusions are conditional on these constraints.

Results

The dependent variable percentage of vote Remain (henceforth RemainPcnt) is positively correlated with the independent variables tested in this study: Globalism–Nationalism (henceforth GlobNat), Economism–Populism (henceforth EconPop), and RemainLeave, i.e., support for either campaign measured by advocacy hashtags ($r = .31$, .46, and .26, respectively). The independent variable GlobNat refers to the polarity Globalism and Nationalism, in which a message with the highest Globalist content is rated 1 and a message with the highest Nationalist content is rated 0. The same scale applies to the variable EconPop, with the polarities Economism and Populism varying between 1 and 0, and RemainLeave, which is the average affiliation calculated per user, also normalized to a scale of 1 to the Remain campaign and 0 to the Leave campaign.

We approach hypothesis H1 by exploring the similitude between the geographic distribution of politically charged tweets and the geography of the vote, aggregated to the level of Parliamentary Constituencies. As detailed in the Methods section, we relied on hashtags unequivocally advocating either side of the campaign to generate a vector varying from 0 (total Leave support) to 1 (total Remain support). This variable (RemainLeave) is significantly correlated with the results of the vote ($r = .26$. $p < .0001$), but upon regressing the referendum results variable (RemainPcnt) on this explanatory variable, we found that it can explain a modest 6% of the variance found in the data ($R^2_{adj} = .068$, $p = 2.377e{-}11$). Therefore, we reject hypothesis H1 and conclude that the spread of hashtags advocating either side of the campaign is a poor predictor of the referendum outcome at granular levels such as Parliamentary Constituencies.

Next we tested hypotheses H2 and H3 by investigating whether the distribution of Nationalistic and Globalist tweets mirrored the distribution of Remain and Leave vote across Constituencies. The two explanatory variables are significantly correlated with the results of the referendum ($r = .31$ and .46, for GlobNat and EconPop, respectively, $p < .0001$), but it is the results of the regression that are particularly interesting. While the polarity Globalism–Nationalism has a modest albeit significant explanatory power ($R^2_{adj} = .10$, $p = 9.226e{-}16$), the polarity Economism–Populism explains over one-fifth of the variance found in the results of the referendum ($R^2_{adj} = .21$, $p < 2.2e{-}16$). Figure 3 shows how the classifier positioned each of the half-a-million tweets processed in this study with the fitted line representing the trend detected by the algorithm.

The classifier reported a strong nationalist sentiment in the data, which persists throughout the campaign and is only offset in the last days when a globalist upsurge brings the British Twittersphere closer to an equally partitioned divide between nationalism and globalism. For most of the campaign, the overall sentiment is decidedly nationalistic averaging .40, which translates to three quarters of messages having a nationalistic sentiment. On the Economism vs. Populism spectrum, the sentiment is reversed: most messages tweeted in the period (61%) are preoccupied with economic implications and opportunities presented by the vote to leave the EU. Though messages with a strong populist

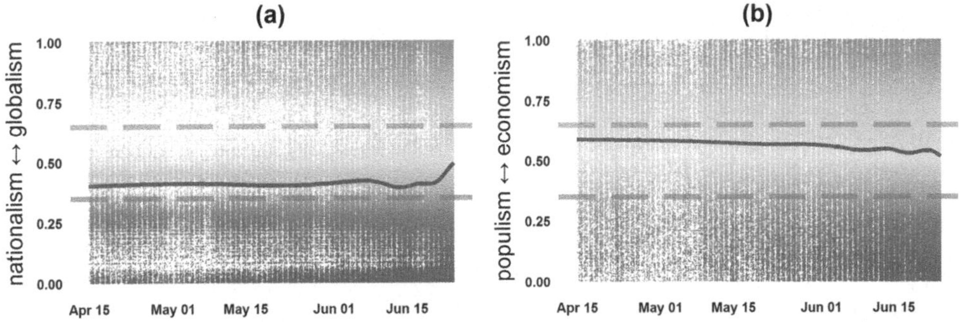

Figure 3. Ideological value space calculated from Twitter messages. Blue line indicates the probability of nationalist versus globalist (a) and populist versus economist (b) sentiments, respectively. Plotted dots indicate the position of each of the half million messages.

appeal account for less than 40% of the total messages, the trend shown in Figure 3 is of growing occurrence of populist messages in the weeks and days leading up to the vote, with messages centred on economic issues moving out of the debate as a populist discussion balloons.

Lastly, we test hypothesis H4 that the ideological value space can be combined with demographic variables to model public opinion formation relative to the referendum results (multiple regression model). We begin by regressing the vote results on the variables RemainLeave (support with vocal hashtags), the variables GlobNat and EconPop generated by the classifier, and the percentage of the population that is economically active in each Parliamentary Constituency. Except for GlobNat, all variables are deemed significant and the model explains about one quarter of the variance found in the results of the referendum (see Table 1). Next, we include a range of demographic variables and perform a stepwise model selection by Akaike Information Criterion (AIC). The returned stepwise-selected model includes an ANOVA component that rejects the variable GlobNat (due to low significance) and incorporates the variables unemployment, valid votes, electorate, and retired population, which unsurprisingly much improve the model. Electorate size and valid votes are variables that favour urban areas (apart from London) where Twitter penetration is considerably higher (Pew Research Center, 2013), while economic variables such as unemployment and size of the retired population have been found to be associated with vote Leave (Becker et al., 2016).

When combined with the political value space mapped with Twitter messages, the model that incorporates demographic data accounts for nearly half of the variance found in the referendum results ($R^2_{\text{adj}} = .41$, $p < 2.2\text{e}{-16}$). Table 1 shows that this model offers a considerable improvement over the previous model, which lacked demographic data, and foregrounds the possibilities of complex social data modelling by mixing social media signal with demographic data that can be aggregated at user, group, or community levels. Although social media data remain a non-representative sample of the larger population, they can provide important markers for understanding the evolution of public debates and the geographic coverage of the discussion (Bastos, Recuero, & Zago, 2014). The results of the classifier also shed light on the importance of economic issues that might have been of vital importance to the user base tweeting the referendum, a

Table 1. Models incorporating demographic variables, such as unemployment and economically active population, with the ideological value space on Twitter to explain the referendum results.

(a)				
Residuals:				
Min	1Q	Median	3Q	Max
−0.30132	−0.06142	0.01312	0.07234	0.23328
Coefficients:				
	Estimate	Std. Error	*t* value	Pr(>|*t*|)
(Intercept)	3.664170	1.162669	3.152	0.00170**
RemainLeave	−4.255821	2.525347	−1.685	0.09244
GlobNat	0.124783	0.327011	0.382	0.70290
EconPop	−1.540038	0.173522	−8.875	<2e−16***
econActivePcnt	−0.003563	0.001174	−3.035	0.00251**
(b)				
Residuals:				
Min	1Q	Median	3Q	Max
−0.298907	−0.052397	0.008676	0.061566	0.225134
Coefficients:				
	Estimate	Std. error	*t* value	Pr(>|*t*|)
(Intercept)	1.915e+00	5.156e−01	3.714	0.000222***
RemainLeave	−2.385e+00	1.092e+00	−2.183	0.029404*
EconPop	−9.355e−01	1.400e−01	−6.681	5.26e−11***
unempPcnt	2.734e−02	3.444e−03	7.939	9.50e−15***
Valid_Votes	1.975e−06	3.963e−07	4.984	8.09e−07***
Electorate	−1.453e−06	2.722e−07	−5.339	1.31e−07***
econInactiveRetiredPcnt	1.318e−02	1.139e−03	11.570	<2e−16***

Signif. codes*(a)*:
0 '***' 0.001 '**' 0.01 '*' 0.05 '.' 0.1 ' ' 1
Residual standard error: 0.1004 on 625 degrees of freedom
Multiple *R*-squared: 0.2317, Adjusted *R*-squared: 0.2268
F-statistic: 47.12 on 4 and 625 DF, *p*-value: <2.2e−16
Signif. codes*(b)*:
0 '***' 0.001 '**' 0.01 '*' 0.05 '.' 0.1 ' ' 1
Residual standard error: 0.08802 on 623 degrees of freedom
Multiple *R*-squared: 0.4112, Adjusted *R*-squared: 0.4055
F-statistic: 72.52 on 6 and 623 DF, *p*-value: <2.2e−16.

component of the Brexit debate overshadowed by the much-discussed cleavage between the metropolitan elite in London and parts of England and Wales that were economically worse off.

However, these results only partially support hypothesis H4—that the ideological value space can be used to model public opinion formation relative to the referendum results. More than half of the variance found in the referendum results remain unaccounted by the model and a closer inspection of the aggregate scores for Globalism, Nationalism, Economism, and Populism show that the map only partially matches the results of the referendum (Figure 4c). Apart from London and north-west Wales (Gwynedd), globalist messages are absent in Figure 4a, with nationalist content appearing in Scotland (which voted Remain, but has long contended with a nationalistic agenda pressing for an independent Scotland), the English Midlands, and the north of England. Populist messages are also relatively underwhelming covering only portions of the Midlands and North (Figure 4b). It is the economic discourse that is prevalent in the debate registered in the Twittersphere, being particularly prominent in Scotland, north-west Wales, and Greater London (Figure 4b). As an expression of the public opinion, Twitter debate appears invariably focused on economic and nationalistic issues as opposed to the

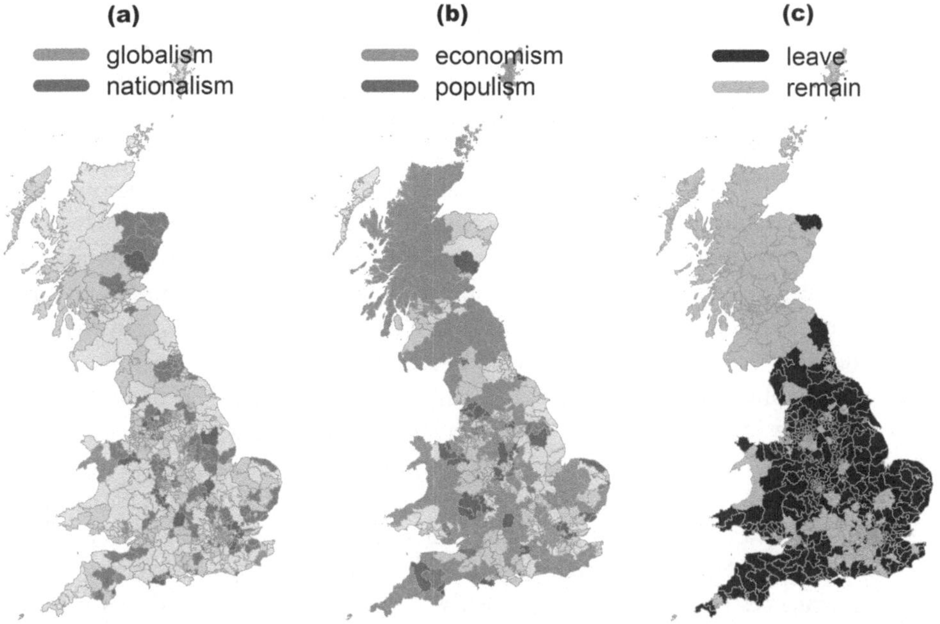

Figure 4. Mean score of Globalism–Nationalism (a) and Economism–Populism (b) for each Parliamentary Constituency and the results of the referendum (c).

populist and globalist sentiments thought to have shaped much of the referendum campaign (Inglehart & Norris, 2016).

Discussion and conclusion

The results reported in this study have partially upset our expectations. We did not find, for one, that economically fragile northern Britain was any more likely to embrace nationalist content. In fact, it was Scotland that appeared as a relatively fertile ground for nationalist messages. Furthermore, we rejected hypothesis H1, which posited that the distribution of users using hashtags to advocate either side of the campaign would mirror the results of the referendum. These results contradict previous research that found the expression of agreement with a topic on Twitter to predict the results of the referendum (Celli et al., 2016)—at least at more granular levels such as Parliamentary Constituencies. Although hypotheses H2 and H3 are partially supported, the distribution of globalist, nationalist, populist, and economist content is somewhat at odds with the geographic distribution of the Leave-Remain vote. More importantly, the significant results reported with the model tested for hypothesis H4 relies heavily on the AIC stepwise model selection that incorporated variables exogenous to the Twitter network such as unemployment, valid votes, electorate, and ratio of retired population living in the constituency.

Twitter conversation in the weeks leading up to the referendum vote was largely centred on nationalistic and economic sentiments, a result that sheds light on the central research question investigated in this study—i.e., that not only material inequality, but also ideological realignments have contributed to the outcome of the referendum. On the one hand, the variables that have improved the model are associated with issues surrounding material inequality, chief of which are the percentage of economically active residents and the size of the parliamentary constituency. On the other hand, ideological orientation has also proven capable of explaining the unexpected outcome of the UK public to leave the EU. As such, our results suggest that it was primarily outrage at material inequality along with a nationalistic upsurge that can help explain this epochal change in British politics (Inglehart & Norris, 2016), a result somewhat at odds with literature foregrounding the resurgence of populism in Western industrialized countries (Tollefson, 2016).

In summary, we found evidence that nationalism was a quintessential component of the referendum debate during most of the campaign, with three quarters of messages having some degree of nationalistic sentiment embedded in them. These results however need to be considered in the context of the limited heuristic value of this ideological coordinate. While the classifier successfully identifies nationalistic sentiments in Scotland and the Midlands, these areas have voiced fundamentally different versions of nationalism. In other words, although nationalism appears to have been a critical marker of the Brexit value space, there are important differences in Scottish and English nationalism that extrapolate the heuristic confines of the classifier. Populist messages, however, were decidedly of lesser importance compared with the sheer volume of tweets discussing the economic consequences and opportunities of Britain leaving the EU, a trend that is however inverted as we approach the date of the vote.

With this paper, we aimed to advance a proof of concept research design employing social media signal to model the ideological value underpinning the Brexit referendum outcome. The continuous streaming of Twitter messages can be leveraged to identify short and long-term shifts that are difficult to detect with surveys and interview instruments. As such, the rationale of the methodology advanced in this study is to employ social media data as geographically rich intelligence that can be explored and combined with established social science research methods. The strength of the approach explored herewith lies less in its predictive or forecasting power (Jungherr et al., 2012; Jungherr & Jürgens, 2013; Lazer et al., 2009) and more on the range of possibilities for exploring ongoing developments that would otherwise require the extensive, continuous, and expensive use of survey methodologies.

Our analysis is notably restricted to the period of the campaign, with no insights as to how the debate evolved following the referendum. The data were also aggregated both at the geographic level (Parliamentary Constituencies) and on the temporal scale (no longitudinal variance was measured or incorporated into the model). Future research should explore the temporal variation of ideological coordinates that can be continuously mined and detected with a machine learning algorithm such as the one trained for this study. While the fitted model presented herewith has limited explanatory power relative to the outcome of the referendum, greater variability in the opinions of users tweeting campaigns in the run-up to the vote could potentially be detected with such an approach. The temporal component of social media data could also be integrated into the model to explore relationships that might not have been possible to measure otherwise. In short, the results of this study present important insights into the reasons why the British public decided to end the country's membership of the EU, but future research should seek to further investigate the sentiments and ideological positioning that might have crystallized through the referendum debate.

Disclosure statement

No potential conflict of interest was reported by the authors.

Funding

This work was supported by the Research Pump-Priming Fund of the School of Arts and Social Sciences of City, University of London.

Notes on contributors

Marco Bastos is Lecturer in Media and Communication in the Department of Sociology at City, University of London and an affiliate of Duke University's Network Analysis Center.

Dan Mercea is Senior Lecturer in the Department of Sociology at City, University of London. He is the author of *Civic Participation in Contentious Politics: The Digital Foreshadowing of Protest.*

ORCID

Marco Bastos http://orcid.org/0000-0003-0480-1078

References

Anstead, N., & O'Loughlin, B. (2015). Social media analysis and public opinion: The 2010 UK general election. *Journal of Computer-Mediated Communication*, *20*(2), 204–220. doi:10.1111/jcc4.12102

Asthana, A., Quinn, B., & Mason, R. (2016). UK votes to leave EU after dramatic night divides nation, *The Guardian*. Retrieved from https://www.theguardian.com/politics/2016/jun/24/britain-votes-for-brexit-eu-referendum-david-cameron

Bakshy, E., Messing, S., & Adamic, L. (2015). Exposure to ideologically diverse news and opinion on Facebook. *Science*, *348*(6239), 1130–1132. doi:10.1126/science.aaa1160

Barberá, P., Jost, J. T., Nagler, J., Tucker, J. A., & Bonneau, R. (2015). Tweeting from left to right: Is online political communication more than an echo chamber? *Psychological Science*, *26*(10), 1531–1542. doi:10.1177/0956797615594620

Bastos, M. T., & Mercea, D. (2017). The Brexit Botnet and user-generated hyperpartisan news. *Social Science Computer Review*, doi:10.1177/0894439317734157

Bastos, M. T., Recuero, R. C., & Zago, G. S. (2014). Taking tweets to the streets: A spatial analysis of the vinegar protests in Brazil. *First Monday*, *19*(3), doi:10.5210/fm.v19i3.5227

Bauman, Z. (2012). *Liquid modernity*. Cambridge: Polity.

BBC. (2016). EU Referendum: The result in maps and charts. *BBC News*. Retrieved from http://www.bbc.co.uk/news/uk-politics-36616028

Becker, S,O, Fetzer, T., & Novy, D. (2016). *Who voted for Brexit? A comprehensive district-level analysis (pp. 1–69)*. Coventry: Centre for Competitive Advantage in the Global Economy, University of Warwick.

Celli, F., Stepanov, E. A., Poesio, M., & Riccardi, G. (2016). *Predicting Brexit: Classifying agreement is better than sentiment and pollsters*. Paper presented at the workshop on computational modeling of People's Opinions, Personality, and Emotions in Social Media (PEOPLES), Osaka, Japan.

Crouch, C. (1997). The terms of the Neo-liberal consensus. *The Political Quarterly*, *68*(4), 352–360.

Cummings, D. (2016). *On the referendum #20: The campaign, physics, and data science – vote leave's 'Voter Intention Collection System' (VICS) now available for all.* Retrieved from https://dominiccummings.wordpress.com/2016/10/29/on-the-referendum-20-the-campaign-physics-and-data-science-vote-leaves-voter-intention-collection-system-vics-now-available-for-all/

Dahlgren, P. (2009). *Media and political engagement: Citizen, communication and press.* Cambridge: Cambridge University Press.

Dunleavy, P., & Margetts, H. (2001). From majoritarian to pluralist democracy? *Journal of Theoretical Politics, 13*(3), 295–319. doi:10.1177/095169280101300304

Dutton, W. H., Reisdorf, B. C., Dubois, E., & Blank, G. (2017). A cross-national survey of search and politics (March 31, 2017). *Quello Center working paper no. 2944191.* Retrieved from https://ssrn.com/abstract=2944191

Fletcher, R., & Nielsen, R. K. (2017, June 21). Using social media appears to diversify your news diet, not narrow it. *NiemanLab.*

Habermas, J. (1991). *The structural transformation of the public sphere: An inquiry into a category of Bourgeois Society.* Cambridge: MIT Press.

Hanretty, C. (2017). Areal interpolation and the UK's referendum on EU membership. *Journal of Elections, Public Opinion and Parties, 4*, 466–483.

Huyen Do, V., Thomas-Agnan, C., & Vanhems, A. (2015). Spatial reallocation of areal data – another look at basic methods. *Revue D'Économie Régionale & Urbaine, mai*, (1), 58. doi:10.3917/reru.151.0027.

Inglehart, R. F., & Norris, P. (2016). *Trump, Brexit, and the Rise of Populism: Economic have-nots and cultural backlash.* Paper presented at the American Political Science Association Annual Meeting, Philadelphia, USA. https://research.hks.harvard.edu/publications/getFile.aspx?Id = 1401

Jungherr, A., & Jürgens, P. (2013, October 23–26). *Forecasting the pulse: How deviations from regular patterns in online data can identify offline phenomena.* Paper presented at the internet research 14.0, Denver, USA.

Jungherr, A., Jürgens, P., & Schoen, H. (2012). Why the pirate party Won the German election of 2009 or The trouble with predictions: A response to Tumasjan, A., Sprenger, T. O., Sander, P. G., & Welpe, I. M. "predicting elections with Twitter: What 140 characters reveal about political sentiment". *Social Science Computer Review, 30*(2), 229–234. doi:10.1177/0894439311404119

Kriesi, H., & Frey, T. (2008). The United Kingdom: Moving parties in a stable configuration. In E. Grande, H. Kriesi, M. Dolezal, R. Lachat, S. Bornschier, & T. Frey (Eds.), *West European politics in the Age of globalization* (pp. 183–207). Cambridge: Cambridge University Press.

Kriesi, H., Grande, E., Lachat, R., Dolezal, M., Bornschier, S., & Frey, T. (2008). Globalization and its impact on national spaces of competition. In E. Grande, H. Kriesi, M. Dolezal, R. Lachat, S. Bornschier, & T. Frey (Eds.), *West European politics in the Age of globalization* (pp. 3–22). Cambridge: Cambridge University Press.

Laclau, E. (2005). *On populist reason.* London: Verso.

Lazer, D., Pentland, A., Adamic, L., Aral, S., Barabási, A.-L., Brewer, D., & Van Alstyne, M. (2009). Computational social science. *Science, 323*(5915), 721–723. doi:10.1126/science.1167742.

McLaren, L. M. (2002). Public support for the European Union: Cost/benefit analysis or perceived cultural threat? *The Journal of Politics, 64*(2), 551–566.

Mudde, C. (2000). *The ideology of the extreme right.* Manchester: Manchester University Press.

Mudde, C. (2004). The populist zeitgeist. *Government and Opposition, 39*(4), 541–563. doi:10.1111/j.1477-7053.2004.00135.x.

Mudde, C., & Rovira Kaltwasser, C. (2012). *Populism in Europe and the Americas.* Cambridge: Cambridge University Press.

Nilsson, B., & Carlsson, E. (2014). Swedish politicians and new media: Democracy, identity and populism in a digital discourse. *New Media & Society, 16*(4), 655–671. doi:10.1177/1461444813487964.

ONS. (2011). 2011 *Census.* Retrieved from https://www.ons.gov.uk/census/2011census

ONS Geography. (2017). *NHS Postcode Directory User Guide.* Retrieved from https://digital.nhs.uk/media/553/User-guide/pdf/user_guide

ONS Geography. (2011). *National statistics postcode lookup UK.* In O. F. N. Statistics (Ed.). London: ONS.

Parker, G. (2016 12 December). Nigel Farage: Eurosceptic scourge of the 'political elite'. *Financial Times.* Retrieved from https://www.ft.com/content/ab8b3b98-be3a-11e6-8b45-b8b81dd5d080

Pew Research Center. (2013). *The demographics of social media users, 2012*. In M. Duggan & J. Brenner (Eds.). Washington, DC: Pew Research Center's Internet & American Life Project.

Piketty, T. (2014). *Capital in the twenty-first century*. Cambridge MA: The Belknap Press of Harvard University Press.

Rennie Short, J. (2016). The geography of Brexit: What the vote reveals about disunited kingdom. *The Conversation*. Retrieved from http://theconversation.com/the-geography-of-brexit-what-the-vote-reveals-about-the-disunited-kingdom-61633

Selivanov, D. (2016). *text2vec: Modern Text Mining Framework for R (Version 0.4.0): CRAN*. Retrieved from https://CRAN.R-project.org/package=text2vec

Sunstein, C. R. (2007). *Republic.com 2.0*. Princeton, NJ: Princeton University Press.

Tollefson, J. (2016). Researchers baffled by nationalist surge. *Nature*, *540*(7632), 182–183. doi:10.1038/540182a.

Tumasjan, A., Sprenger, T., Sandner, P., & Welpe, I. (2011). Election forecasts with Twitter: How 140 characters reflect the political landscape. *Social Science Computer Review*, doi:citeulike-article-id:8506921

Turner, B. (2002). *Orientalism, postmodernism and globalism*. Singapore: Routledge.

Wills, J. (2015). Populism, localism and the geography of democracy. *Geoforum; Journal of Physical, Human, and Regional Geosciences*, *62*, 188–189. https://doi.org/10.1016/j.geoforum.2015.04.006.

Woods, D. (2009). Pockets of resistance to globalization: The case of the Lega Nord. *Patterns of Prejudice*, *43*(2), 161–177.

2 Facebook news and (de)polarization

Reinforcing spirals in the 2016 US election

Michael A. Beam, Myiah J. Hutchens and Jay D. Hmielowski

ABSTRACT

The rise of social media, and specifically Facebook, as a dominant force in the flow of news in the United States has led to concern that people incur greater isolation from diverse perspectives through filter bubbles (from algorithmic filtering) and echo chambers (from an information environment populated by social recommendations coming from overwhelmingly like-minded others). This evolution in news diffusion comes at a time when Americans report increased affective partisan polarization. In particular, evidence shows increasingly negative attitudes about out-party members. Based on selective exposure and reinforcing spirals model perspectives, we examined the reciprocal relationship between Facebook news use and polarization using national 3-wave panel data collected during the 2016 US Presidential Election. Over the course of the campaign, we found media use and attitudes remained relatively stable. Our results also showed that Facebook news use was related to a modest over-time spiral of depolarization. Furthermore, we found that people who use Facebook for news were more likely to view both pro- and counter-attitudinal news in each wave. Our results indicated that counter-attitudinal news exposure increased over time, which resulted in depolarization. We found no evidence of a parallel model, where pro-attitudinal exposure stemming from Facebook news use resulted in greater affective polarization.

Facebook continues its rise as a dominant online distribution platform with about half of US adults reporting using the site for news in 2016 (Gottfried & Shearer, 2016). The rise of social media has realigned the flow of news such that news stories are often filtered through social and algorithmic recommendation systems instead of traditional editorial news gatekeepers. Simultaneously, changes in the US media system coupled with the proliferation of partisan news sources in recent decades have resulted in increased political polarization (Hmielowski, Beam, & Hutchens, 2016). Taken together, an increase in partisan content and changes in the flow of news information has led some scholars to worry that social media will exacerbate polarization by promoting echo chambers and filter bubbles (Pariser, 2011; Sunstein, 2017).

Selective exposure research has long-guided debates about people's tendencies to engage in attitude-reinforcing news exposure (Donsbach & Mothes, 2012; Stroud, 2014). Much of the research on the new paradigm of social media news flow has adopted this theoretical lens, trying to determine if partisan tendencies are amplified through social newsfeeds. This empirical research has found that increased choice does not necessarily result in decreased exposure to counter-attitudinal ideas (Bakshy, Messing, & Adamic, 2015; Beam, 2014; Flaxman, Goel, & Rao, 2016; Messing & Westwood, 2014). Our study aims to extend these findings by investigating the role of using social media recommendations on partisan attitudes.

To understand the process tied to selective exposure in an over-time context, we employ Slater's (2007, 2015) reinforcing spirals model (RSM). The RSM provides a theoretical extension of selective exposure where social identity, in this case partisan identity, leads to identity-consistent information exposure over time resulting in three possible attitudinal outcomes: polarization, depolarization, or homeostasis. That is, if people rely on news generated by social and algorithmic filters on social media, they may view greater pro-attitudinal news and be relatively isolated from counter-attitudinal news resulting in increased polarization. Conversely, filtered social media recommendations might drive greater news engagement for social media users compared to non-users, resulting in more exposure and understanding regarding both pro- and counter-attitudinal arguments. Depending on how people process counter-attitudinal news, this latter process could result in depolarization—due to greater understanding of competing viewpoints or less confidence in their own attitudes—or homeostasis, where pre-existing attitudes remain reinforced, but unchanged over time.

This study adopts the RSM framework to investigate the over-time effect of Facebook news use on attitude polarization during the contentious 2016 US Presidential Election. Specifically, we examine the over-time relationship between Facebook news use and affective polarization. We extend this model by subsequently examining whether Facebook news use is associated with seeing attitude consistent or inconsistent information during the course of the election campaign. We test the indirect over-time effects of Facebook news use on attitude (de)polarization through pro- and counter-attitudinal news exposure. To test these models, we use YouGov data collected during the course of the 2016 Presidential Election.

Rising political polarization in the United States

Within the US, scholars and pundits have become concerned about the increasing levels of polarization within the country. Scholars have tracked the ideological gap between Democrats and Republicans in the House and Senate showing the parties (especially the Republican Party) becoming more ideologically extreme (McCarty, Poole, & Rosenthal, 2016). Research has followed to understand what factors among voters could be driving the increasing ideological gap in Congress. Some scholars have argued that the increasing ideological gap in Congress reflects the increasing attitudinal gaps between Democratic and Republican voters on controversial issues such as gun control, abortion, and gay marriage (Abramowitz & Saunders, 2008). Others have found few changes in attitude polarization over time within the US (Fiorina, Abrams, & Pope, 2011). More recently, scholars have focused on the concept of affective polarization (Abramowitz, 2010; Iyengar, Sood, &

Lelkes, 2012). Affective polarization has been described as increasing negative feelings or emotions that people feel toward the opposing political party (Abramowitz, 2010; Iyengar et al., 2012). In other words, affective polarization is when Democrats increasingly dislike Republicans, and Republicans increasingly dislike Democrats.

There are a variety of explanations for increasing levels of affective polarization in the US including increased money in politics (Lessig, 2011), elite polarization (McCarty et al., 2016), and a fragmented media environment (Hmielowski et al., 2016; Iyengar et al., 2012; Lelkes, Sood, & Iyengar, 2017). Regarding the latter explanation, changes in the media system as a result of deregulation of media ownership (Hmielowski et al., 2016) coupled with the rise of the Internet (Lelkes et al., 2017) has meant citizens can access significantly more news sources now than ever before. As the number of news sources has proliferated, many news organizations have focused on more narrow and partisan news audiences (Prior, 2013). News organizations like the conservative FOX News and Breitbart News and the liberal MSNBC and Huffington Post have connected with niche audiences that align with their political worldview (Benkler, Faris, Roberts, & Zuckerman, 2017). Indeed, scholars have found that over the last 30 years those who pay more attention to TV news have reported rising levels of affective polarization compared to those who do not watch news (Hmielowski et al., 2016). Scholars have noted that social media newsfeeds may also be contributing to increasing levels of affective polarization (Sunstein, 2017). People who are strong partisans are more likely to share news on social media (Weeks & Holbert, 2013), potentially creating a highly partisan information environment. Plus, there is evidence that Facebook's proprietary algorithm favors pro-attitudinal news stories over other types of media content (e.g., counter-attitudinal news) (Bakshy et al., 2015; Tufekci, 2015). If users are exposed to primarily pro-attitudinal information due to their social and algorithmic recommendations, they might polarize over time. Lelkes and his colleagues (2017) argued that online selective exposure is a probable driver of their finding that access to broadband internet was related to increased partisan affective polarization. However, there is still debate and competing evidence among selective exposure researchers about the role of social media relative to the media content people choose to consume.

Media choice and selective exposure

People's selective exposure to particular partisan information has been frequently cited as a theoretical mechanism for understanding media's contribution to the increasingly polarized electorate. Selective exposure research often finds theoretical roots in cognitive dissonance theory, which posits that people are likely to choose attitude-consistent information over attitude-inconsistent information (Stroud, 2014). Under this theoretical perspective, people in a more fragmented and partisan media environment would likely be exposed to more attitude-consistent information. There is ample evidence from decades of research that people generally select attitude-consistent information, but there is less evidence that people avoid attitude-dissonant information (Garrett, Carnahan, & Lynch, 2013). Based on these mixed findings, scholars have actively debated the effects of partisan news sources, social recommendations, and algorithmic filters on information exposure and political attitudes (Beam, 2014; Donsbach & Mothes, 2012; Dylko et al., 2018; Garrett et al., 2013; Sunstein, 2017).

Social media, filter bubbles, and echo chambers

There are several reasons that the internet has been implicated in the rise of polarization through selective exposure research. First, the internet has a vast amount of information relative to other media platforms (Andrejevic, 2013). Second, the economy of the internet is largely based on personalized information tailored to individual users. The most prosperous technology companies including Google, Amazon, and Facebook have been successful by providing users with personalized search, consumer, and social information tailored to their specific profile (Pariser, 2011). Third, people are less likely to rely on specific sources for news. Instead, people are increasingly consuming news content on social newsfeeds populated by social and algorithmic recommendations (Gil de Zúñiga, Weeks, & Ardèvol-Abreu, 2017). These changes in news information flow have led scholars and journalists to voice concern that social media is promoting filter bubbles where people are isolated from news due to personalized filtering and echo chambers where people are increasingly surrounded by information shared from like-minded friends and acquaintances (Pariser, 2011; Sunstein, 2017).

Filter bubbles and echo chambers have negative implications for ideal normative citizenship and a properly functioning democracy. Ideal citizenship in a democracy requires people to engage in politics after gathering information from diverse sources and disparate viewpoints in order to make a decision based on factual information. Of course, this normative bar is unrealistic, as citizens have generally demonstrated relatively low amounts of political information seeking and knowledge (Delli-Carpini & Keeter, 1996; Prior, 2007). Critics of social media's algorithmic and social recommendations have worried that these technologies will foster isolation from counter-attitudinal information, hindering people's ability to make a good decision (Sunstein, 2017). A natural consequence of viewing biased, one-sided information is a highly polarized electorate that elects highly polarized representatives. As a result, democratic institutions fail to deal with key issues hindering progress in a society.

Fortunately, counter to these concerns, research on internet users has consistently found a positive relationship between pro- and counter-attitudinal news exposure. Studies using a variety of methods have shown that people using the internet and social media are not shielded from counter-attitudinal news (Bakshy et al., 2015; Beam, 2014; Flaxman et al., 2016; Garrett, 2009; Garrett & Stroud, 2014; Gentzkow & Shapiro, 2011; Messing & Westwood, 2014). In fact, people who use online recommendations for news and social media for politics show higher levels of structural political knowledge and political participation (Beam, Hutchens, & Hmielowski, 2016; Yamamoto, Kushin, & Dalisay, 2015). Despite the progress made on this topic, scholars have spent less time examining the theoretical link between social media news use and attitude polarization over time. This study aims to contribute to this ongoing debate about the role of social media recommendations by testing a RSM that integrates selective exposure and over-time media effects (Slater, 2007, 2015).

(De)Polarization through reinforcing spirals

The RSM perspective builds on selective exposure by theorizing over-time attitudinal effects and media exposure in which people's identities and attitudes are reinforced (Slater,

2007, 2015). Slater (2007) argues that communication research needs to account for over-time changes in theoretically important variables to better understand media effects. Furthermore, this perspective emphasizes that communication variables are often theoretically reciprocally related, rather than associated in a simple cause-and-effect order. Slater (2015) argues this is especially true in the context of election campaigns, when two competing partisan identities are made salient. When thinking about the relationship between social media use and political polarization, the three potential over-time outcomes are partisan polarization, partisan depolarization, or homeostasis (stable partisan attitudes).

Donsbach and Mothes (2012) adopt the reinforcing spirals perspective in arguing that selective technologies are reciprocally related to polarization and depolarization through a process of pro- and counter-attitudinal exposure. According to the RSM, the reinforcing process can start with either media exposure or partisan attitudes, as the two will have a reciprocal influence on each other. The theoretical link for why individuals may depolarize over time can be seen through the research stream that examines exposure to a variety of sources. In general, the research focused on interpersonal communication has frequently argued that counter-attitudinal information leads to more understanding and greater tolerance for other people's perspectives (Mutz, 2006) and is associated with weaker attitudes (Bello & Rolfe, 2013; Mutz, 2006). Specifically related to polarization, in interpersonal contexts Kim (2015) found that exposure to counter-attitudinal information was associated with lower levels of affective polarization. Researchers looking at the diversity of information that individuals consume has found that seeking a wider range of opinions is associated with weaker attitudes (Hmielowski, 2012). For example, increased attitudinal ambivalence (i.e., a weaker attitude) has been observed in those who consume more counter-attitudinal mediated information (Donsbach & Mothes, 2012; Hmielowski, Beam, & Hutchens, 2017). Given that research consistently has shown that individuals do see counter-attitudinal views in news feeds (Bakshy et al., 2015; Beam, 2014; Flaxman et al., 2016; Garrett, 2009; Garrett & Stroud, 2014; Gentzkow & Shapiro, 2011; Messing & Westwood, 2014), this would suggest that social media news use could result in depolarization. In fact, Boxell and his colleagues (2017) found that those who use the internet and social media the least showed the greatest gains in polarization using rolling cross-sectional data between 1996 and 2006. Similarly, Holmes and McNeal (2016) found that social media users (coded using a binary measure of SNS use) showed attenuated partisan polarization in survey data collected before and after the 2012 US Election. In contrast, Lelkes and his colleagues (2017) found that broadband internet availability was related to increased polarization using survey data from 2004 to 2008. This study builds upon this past scholarship by testing the relationship between frequency of social media news use and (de)polarization during a campaign using the reinforcing spirals theoretical lens. Using this theory, we are able to test a process where online news exposure mediates the relationship between social media news use and affective political polarization.

Donsbach and Mothes (2012) suggest that a reinforcing spiral of polarization may occur through exposure to attitude-consistent information, using similar theoretical linkages as the depolarization argument. In particular, users might begin a campaign trapped in filter bubbles and echo chambers, where people view overwhelmingly pro-attitudinal news. Some selective exposure research focused on the internet's high choice environment has found evidence of ideological selection. For example, Lawrence and his colleagues

(2010) found that ideological blog users were far more likely to view pro-attitudinal blogs than counter-attitudinal blogs. Experimental work on algorithmic news recommendations has found that users consistently see more pro-attitudinal news than counter-attitudinal news (e.g., Beam, 2014; Dylko et al., 2018). Research has shown that exposure to attitude-consistent information frequently strengthens attitudes (Dylko et al., 2018; Garrett et al., 2014), which could cause attitudes to polarize resulting in greater subsequent selectivity. The research on affective polarization mentioned already has clearly shown that polarization and selective processes have occurred over the past decades (e.g., Hmielowski et al., 2016; Lelkes et al., 2017).

Using technology to read news might result in media consumption that stays relatively stable over time. In this latter case, termed homeostasis, existing attitudes may be reinforced, but attitude changes may not occur over time. Essentially, while attitudes can change, they are, in fact, relatively stable. Slater argues that media use is often used to reinforce and maintain rather than change attitudes (2015).

To date, few studies have empirically investigated attitude change over time in a reinforcing spirals perspective. One recent study from Garrett and his colleagues (2014) found that greater pro-attitudinal exposure results in subsequent polarization and counter-attitudinal exposure results in subsequent depolarization. That is, the more people viewed news online from pro-attitudinal sources, the greater affective polarization they reported in subsequent waves. Similarly, they found some evidence that counter-attitudinal exposure was related to less polarized affective attitudes at a later time. However, they also found that exposure to both pro- and counter-attitudinal sources resulted in greater polarization. These findings are consistent with the partisan identity protection processes described in the RSM. Our findings extend this theoretical debate by focusing specifically on the context of using the social network site Facebook for news, which provides news recommendations through social and algorithmic filtering.

Research question and hypotheses

Our study will test the RSM on affective partisan polarization from Facebook news use in the context of the 2016 US Presidential Election. We first test whether Facebook news use is related to increased or decreased attitude polarization both cross-sectionally (RQ1a) and over time in a reinforcing spiral (RQ1b). Next, we test our proposed theoretical process model, where increased polarization during the campaign stems from a reinforcing link between Facebook news use and pro-attitudinal news exposure (H1). Lastly, we test a theoretical process model, where increased depolarization during the campaign stems from a reinforcing link between Facebook news use and counter-attitudinal news exposure (H2).

Method

This study analyzed nationally representative sample-matched survey data collected from 500 US adults in 3 waves during the 2016 US election collected by the survey firm YouGov. YouGov utilizes a sample-matching procedure, wherein they initially oversample from opt-in participants and then create a final sample that matches national population characteristics. A sampling frame to create the final sample is generated using benchmarks from large, high-quality probability samples. YouGov's sample-matching procedure has been empirically compared to random sampling procedures and found to exhibit little to no selection bias (see Ansolabehere & Rivers, 2013; Ansolabehere & Schaffner, 2014). Indeed, these scholars empirically demonstrated that properly weighted sample-matching procedures generate samples better than other internet panels and are equivalent to the random methods used to create high-quality surveys such as the American National Election Survey. A table comparing our demographics to 2016 US Census data are provided in Table A1 in an online appendix. This sample was created using a sampling frame that matched participants on gender, age, race, education, party identification, ideology, political interest, voter registration, and voter turnout. Weights were provided by YouGov based on propensity scores created via age, gender, race/ethnicity, years of education, and ideology. The first wave of data was collected 11–23 August 2016 after the major party conventions. The second wave was collected 21–28 September 2016 just prior to the Presidential Debates. The third and final wave was collected 24–30 October 2016, after the debates, but prior to Election Day.

Focal variables

Affective polarization

Affective polarization was measured using partisan feeling-thermometer measures (similar to those used in Iyengar et al., 2012; Garrett et al., 2014). Participants were asked to rate how much they liked the Republican Party and the Democratic Party on a 100-point scale. Affective polarization was calculated using the absolute value of the difference between the two scores ($M_{w1} = 50.3$, $SD_{w1} = 31.9$, $M_{w2} = 50.5$, $SD_{w2} = 32.1$, $M_{w3} = 49.1$, $SD_{w3} = 31.5$). Our models, described in more detail below, analyze all three waves of data. To successfully run the models, we needed participants to have values for all waves to run the full process model. To retain a larger sample size, if individuals were just missing one of the three scores for affective party attitudes, we imputed that score by averaging the other two waves, which slightly altered the overall descriptive statistics of the affective polarization scores ($M_{w1} = 49.8$, $SD_{w1} = 32.0$, $M_{w2} = 49.8$, $SD_{w2} = 31.8$, $M_{w3} = 49.8$, $SD_{w3} = 31.4$). An independent samples *t*-test, comparing the polarization scores of those who had an imputed value and those who did not, indicated there were no significant differences between their polarization scores for any of the three waves ($t_{w1}(458) = 1.395$, $p > .05$, $t_{w2}(466) = .312$, $p > .05$, $t_{w3}(464) = .519$, $p > .05$). Pairwise *t*-tests comparing changes in affective polarization show that we do not see any significant changes over time for the general sample, $t_{w1-w2}(454) = .10$, $p = .92$; $t_{w1-w3}(454) = -.01$, $p = .99$; $t_{w2-w3}(454) = -.10$, $p = .92$. In total, 96 individuals had a single thermometer score imputed.

Facebook news use

Facebook news use was measured using two self-reported frequency items. These items included reading headlines in their Facebook newsfeed and clicking on news links shared on Facebook. Responses were coded from 0 (Never) to 5 (Several times a day). A mean score was computed for Facebook news exposure ($M_{w1} = 1.86$, $SD_{w1} = 1.67$, Spearman–Brown coefficient $(S\text{-}B)_{w1} = .86$, $M_{w2} = 1.64$, $SD_{w2} = 1.61$, $S\text{-}B_{w2} = .86$, $M_{w3} = 1.60$, $SD_{w3} = 1.55$, $S\text{-}B_{w3} = .85$). Pairwise *t*-tests comparing changes in Facebook news use show that we see the greatest use of Facebook for news at wave 1, earlier in the campaign,

$t_{w1-w2}(499) = 4.12, p < .001$; $t_{w2} = .86, M_3 = 1.60, SD_{w3} = 1.55$, S-B$_{w3} = .85$). Pairwise t-tests comparing changes in Facebook news use show that we see the greatest use of Facebook for news at wave 1, earlier in the campaign, $t_{w1-w2}(499) = 4.12, p < .001$; $t_{1-w3}(499) = 4.44$, $p < .001$. We see no changes in Facebook news use between the second and third waves of data collection $t_{w2-w3}(499) = .67, p = .51$.

Partisan online news exposure

Partisan online news exposure was measured using two items for both conservative and liberal sources. Again, responses were coded from 0 (Never) to 5 (Several times a day). For conservative sources, participants were asked how often they used 'The website of a major national news organization that is frequently characterized as favoring conservative positions or Republican candidates, such as *The Wall Street Journal* or FOX News' and 'The website of a politically conservative online news organization or blog, such as Drudge Report, TownHall or the Cybercast News Service (CNS News)' ($M_{w1} = 1.30$, $SD_{w1} = 1.35$, S-B$_{w1} = .66$, $M_{w2} = 1.23$, $SD_{w2} = 1.33$, S-B$_{w2} = .71$, $M_{w3} = 1.28$, $SD_{w3} = 1.32$, S-B$_{w3} = .69$). For liberal sources, participants were asked how often they used 'The website of a major national news organization that is frequently characterized as favoring liberal positions or Democratic candidates, such as *The New York Times* or MSNBC' and 'The website of a politically liberal online news organization or blog, such as *Daily Kos* or *Huffington Post*' ($M_{w1} = 1.16$, $SD_{w1} = 1.24$, S-B$_{w1} = .69$, $M_{w2} = 1.25$, $SD_{w2} = 1.61$, S-B$_{w2} = .70$, $M_{w3} = 1.20$, $SD_{w3} = 1.33$, S-B$_{w3} = .73$). Participants' vote preference or lean for Republican Party candidate Donald Trump (conservative) or Democratic Party candidate Hillary Clinton (liberal) determined which type of news use was coded as pro-attitudinal ($M_{w1} = 1.62$, $SD_{w1} = 1.41$, $M_{w2} = 1.61$, $SD_{w2} = 1.39$, $M_{w3} = 1.68$, $SD_{w3} = 1.45$) or counter-attitudinal ($M_{w1} = .86$, $SD_{w1} = 1.08$, $M_{w2} = .83$, $SD_{w2} = 1.09$, $M_{w3} = .84$, $SD_{w3} = 1.04$). Participants who did not indicate a candidate preference were excluded from this analysis ($N = 51$). Pairwise t-tests comparing changes in pro-attitudinal news use show that we do not see any significant changes over time for the general sample, $t_{w1-w2}(460) = .22$, $p = .82$; $t_{w1-w3}(460) = -1.22$, $p = .22$; $t_{w2-w3}(460) = -1.56$, $p = .12$. Similarly, we also do not see changes in counter-attitudinal news use over time for the general sample, $t_{w1-w2}(460) = .55$, $p = .58$; $t_{w1-w3}(460) = .48$, $p = .63$; $t_{w2-w3}(460) = -.10$, $p = .91$.

Control variables

All our analyses control for demographic variables including *age, income, gender, education,* and *race. Age* was measured with a single item, asking participants for their age in years ($M = 46.70$, $SD = 17.52$). *Income* was measured with one item using a 9-point scale that ranged from less than 10,000 dollars a year (coded 0) to more than 150,000 dollars a year (coded 8) ($M = 3.69$, $SD = 2.30$, between \$30k-<\$40k and \$40k-<\$50k). *Gender* was measured with one item asking respondents their biological sex (51.5% female). *Education* was measured with one item using a 9-point scale that ranged from 'None' (coded 0) to 'Post Graduate Training or School' (coded 8) ($M = 4.68$, $SD = 1.94$, between post-secondary vocational school and some college). *Race* was measured by asking participants to identify their ethnicity. They were instructed to select all that apply. We dummy coded participants that selected any race other than 'white' and 'non-Hispanic' as a minority (36% minority). *Political ideology* was also included as a control variable, as some online news studies have found differences amongst liberals and conservatives in their online news behaviors (e.g., Garrett & Stroud, 2014). We asked participants to respond to the statement, 'I would describe my political views as … ' using a scale of 'Very conservative' (coded 0) to 'Very liberal' (coded 6) ($M = 2.66$, $SD = 1.59$). Lastly, we controlled for *political interest.* We asked participants to respond to the statement 'I am very interested in politics,' using a scale of 'Strongly Disagree' (coded 0) to 'Strongly Agree' (coded 6) ($M = 4.23$, $SD = 1.61$).

Analysis plan

Data were tested using lagged path analyses, modeled in Mplus 7, to examine the relationships between our online news use variables and polarization. All models included control variables that were assessed during the first wave of our survey. The models also controlled for the effect of the prior wave's measures of key endogenous variables. For instance, we controlled for Facebook news use at wave 1, when predicting Facebook news use at wave 2. Therefore, the analyses did not use calculated change scores, but rather used the raw scores and accounted for the prior wave's variance. We also correlated our endogenous variables within each wave of data. That is, we correlated Facebook news use, affective polarization, pro-attitudinal online news use and counter-attitudinal online news use with each other in each wave of data. Tables A2 through A7 showing the full model results are available in an online appendix. A lagged path model is preferable to a series of regression models because all of our focal variables can be modeled simultaneously. This treats the model as the process we are proposing rather than a series of disconnected links, and most importantly accounts for all shared variance between our focal variables (Pek & Hoyle, 2016). All coefficients reported are unstandardized. Direct and indirect effects were calculated using a bootstrapping technique with 1000 bootstraps. In these analyses, 95% confidence intervals (CI) that do not cover 0 represent significant results.

One participant was removed from all analyses due to missing data. In our second model, our measures of pro- and counter-attitudinal exposure required individuals to have a candidate preference. Fifty-one individuals did not provide a candidate preference; therefore, the second model presented to test our hypotheses was based on the 449 cases with full data. Analyses were modeled using sample-weights provided by YouGov.

Results

First, we tested a lagged path model that included a reinforcing spiral between Facebook news use and affective political polarization (see Figure 1) to test our research questions. Cross-sectional results showed that during the first wave of data, people who reported higher affective polarization were more likely to view news on Facebook at wave 1 ($B = 6.95$, CI: 2.44 to 11.65). However, we found no significant cross-sectional relationship between Facebook news use and affective polarization in our second or third wave of data (Wave 2: $B = -.01$, CI: −1.97 to 1.90; Wave 3: $B = .43$, CI: −1.85 to 2.81). Therefore, we found only partial evidence that Facebook news use is cross-sectionally related to polarization (RQ1a).

Moving to the over-time analyses illustrated in Figure 1 (RQ1b), results showed that those who were less polarized during the first wave of data collection viewed more news

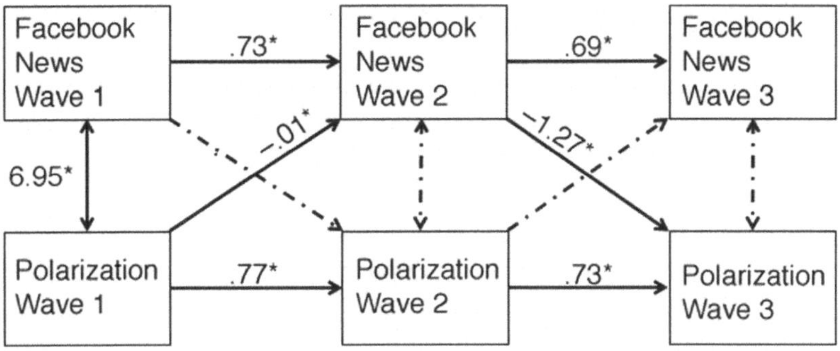

Figure 1. Lagged model of Facebook news use and affective polarization in 2016. Note: Values are unstandardized estimates. Only values for significant paths are displayed.

on Facebook in the second wave ($B = -.01$, CI: −.01 to −.002). Furthermore, those who viewed more news on Facebook in the second wave were less polarized in the third and final wave ($B = -1.27$, CI: −2.54 to −.04). Investigating the indirect effects, we found that Facebook news use in wave 2 mediated decreased polarization between wave 1 and wave 3 ($B = .01$, CI: .001 to .02). Those with lower levels of polarization earlier in the campaign were more likely to show increases in their Facebook news use, which led to over-time depolarization. We do not find significant over-time results when viewing the other paths in the reinforcing spiral. That is, there was no over-time relationship between Facebook news use in wave 1 on polarization in wave 2 ($B = -.38$, CI: −1.47 to .77). And, polarization in wave 2 was unrelated to Facebook news use in wave 3 ($B = .43$, CI: −1.85 to 2.81).

Our next analysis tested a more complex lagged path model that again included Facebook news use, affective polarization, and added pro- and counter-attitudinal online news use to test our hypotheses. Again, we found a cross-sectional relationship between Facebook news use and affective polarization in the first wave of data ($B = 6.88$, CI: 1.92 to 11.06), indicating that those who are more polarized were more likely to turn to Facebook for news at wave 1, earlier in the campaign. Furthermore, our cross-sectional results showed that all waves of Facebook news use were positively related to both pro- (Wave 1: $B = .55$, CI: .37 to .76; Wave 2: $B = .18$, CI: .10 to .28; Wave 3: $B = .27$, CI: .17 to .38) and counter-attitudinal online news use (Wave 1: $B = .37$, CI: .23 to .53; Wave 2: $B = .09$, CI: .01 to .19; Wave 3: $B = .10$, CI: .003 to .20). Consistent with past research on selective avoidance (Garrett et al., 2013), these cross-sectional results indicated that engaging in online news use did not result in isolation from counter-attitudinal news sources.

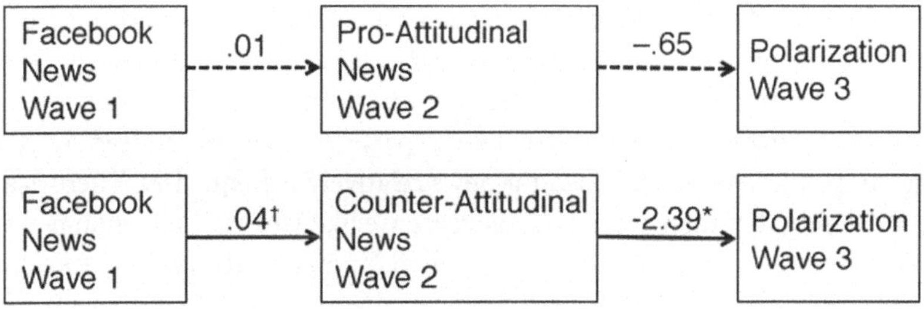

Figure 2. Indirect effects paths proposed in Hypothesis 1 (top) and Hypothesis 2 (bottom). Note: Values are unstandardized estimates.

Figure 2 illustrates the key predicted indirect paths for changes in polarization over time stemming from Facebook news use in our hypotheses. The top illustration in Figure 2 shows that using Facebook for news at wave 1 was unrelated to changes in pro-attitudinal online news use at wave 2 ($B = .01$, CI: −.05 to .06). We also found no relationship between pro-attitudinal news use at wave 2 and affective polarization at wave 3 ($B = -.65$, CI: −2.57 to 1.03). We found no indirect effects between Facebook news use at wave 1 and increased affective polarization at wave 3 mediated by pro-attitudinal news use at wave 2 ($B = -.003$, CI: −.09 to .04). Therefore, we found no support for H1. The bottom illustration in Figure 2 shows that there was a marginal positive relationship between Facebook news use at wave 1 and counter-attitudinal online news use in wave 2 ($B = .04$, 90% CI: .003 to .09). There was a positive relationship between counter-attitudinal news use in wave 2 with decreased affective polarization at wave 3 ($B = -2.39$, CI: −5.19 to −.23). We found indirect effects where Facebook news use at wave 1 resulted in depolarization at wave 3 mediated by counter-attitudinal news at wave 2 ($B = -.10$, CI: −.41 to −.00). Therefore, we found support for H2. In sum, we found modest over-time effects where Facebook news use resulted in depolarization due to increased counter-attitudinal online news exposure.

Discussion

Our analysis tested a RSM to see if use of Facebook, the most popular social media site in the US for news during the 2016 Presidential campaign, was related to selective partisan news exposure and affective polarization, depolarization, or homeostasis. While those who were more politically polarized were more likely to turn to Facebook for news in our first wave of data collection early in the general campaign, we found support for a modest over-time depolarization spiral through reading news on Facebook. Furthermore, a test of a more complex lagged path model including pro- and counter-attitudinal news showed indirect effects from Facebook news use to depolarized affective partisan attitudes occurred due to increased exposure to counter-attitudinal online news sources.

Our study contributes to the literature on social media and politics as it relates to selective exposure, reinforcing spirals, and political polarization. First, our results provide an empirical over-time test of the affective polarization RSM described by Slater (2007, 2015) and Donsbach and Mothes (2012) in the context of social media, where news is presented based on social and algorithmic recommendations. Most importantly, we found no evidence of a partisan reinforcing spiral resulting in increased polarization. Instead, our study shows that Facebook news users who were less polarized at the first wave of data collection were likely to depolarize further due to increased counter-attitudinal exposure. When thinking about the theoretical role of personal identity and identity threat in the RSM, these results indicate that encountering political news in their Facebook newsfeed might activate a 'citizen' identity rather than a 'partisan' identity. Indeed, we found that across our sample, Facebook was used for news relatively infrequently. There is a growing literature indicating that many social media users are likely to stumble upon news incidentally rather than intentionally seeking it out (Gil de Zúñiga et al., 2017; Weeks, Lane, Kim, Lee, & Kwak, 2017).

Similar to past studies on filter bubbles and echo chambers on the internet and social media, we did find evidence for selective exposure to pro-attitudinal information within each wave of data collection. However, like those studies, we also found that use of social media news recommendations resulted in increasing exposure to counter-attitudinal information (Bakshy et al., 2015; Flaxman et al., 2016; Garrett, 2009; Garrett et al., 2014; Garrett & Stroud, 2014; Gentzkow & Shapiro, 2011; Messing & Westwood, 2014). Our results also show that those who reported greater polarization just after the party conventions at wave 1 were less likely to show increases in their Facebook news use over time.

Our study moves beyond past research on social media's polarization effects in our second model, which tested the reinforcing spiral process of depolarization through news exposure. Facebook users showed no over-time increases in pro-attitudinal news exposure compared to non-users. Prior (2013) has argued that the rise in media content due to media fragmentation has resulted in more people choosing to opt out of political information seeking altogether. Therefore, our study indicates that social media might be helping users who are typically less engaged and less motivated by partisan identities to encounter news and engage in the process of political decision-making. Indeed, past research has found that people are more likely to engage in counter-attitudinal exposure and information processing when they receive personalized social and algorithmic recommendations (Anspach, 2017; Beam, 2014; Messing & Westwood, 2014). Based on these arguments, we believe encountering counter-attitudinal news, especially incidentally, on Facebook is the primary driver of our indirect effects on depolarization through counter-attitudinal exposure. Considering our reference group was those who did not use Facebook for news, our evidence indicates that, while counter-attitudinal news exposure is still relatively rare, social, and algorithmic recommendations encourage exposure to diverse ideas. In sum, we expand on past work that finds a depolarizing relationship between social media and partisan attitudes (Boxell, Gentzkow, & Shapiro, 2017; Holmes & McNeal, 2016) by providing evidence of a depolarizing RSM through increased counter-attitudinal exposure. Our findings further debunk the theoretical links between social and algorithmic recommendations of news on social media and filter bubbles and echo chambers.

Furthermore, when looking at the descriptive statistics across each of our endogenous variables we see very little change over time across the sample. Paired-sample *t*-tests showed that affective polarization, pro- and counter-attitudinal online news use remained unchanged across the 3-months we collected data during the campaign. The only difference we found was a small but significant decline in Facebook news use after the first wave of data collection. These results indicate that theoretical changes over time should be hard to detect. In general, we believe more work should be done to investigate the role of homeostasis in communication patterns. While our studies found modest indirect effects on depolarization from those who were less polarized at the outset of the campaign, our first lagged model did not find a reciprocal relationship, where more Facebook news use indirectly led to more Facebook news use. Instead, we found homeostasis when looking at Facebook news use as a dependent variable.

Our study investigates the RSM across our national sample. Future studies with greater statistical power could expand on these findings by adding moderating variables to the reinforcing spiral models. While we control for demographic and political group characteristics in our model, we do not make claims about differential effects from belonging to specific subgroups.

While this study contributes to the scholarly debate about the role of social media in politics, our data present several limitations. We rely on self-reported sample-matched survey data to make our claims. However, as we indicated in our method section, prior studies have tested the quality of YouGov's sample-matching procedures and found it to be less error prone than opt-in national samples and similar in quality of random samples. Furthermore, the exposure and polarization patterns found here are similar to past studies that have utilized large datasets from logged observation data, including studies from Facebook (Bakshy et al., 2015), comScore (Gentzkow & Shapiro, 2011), and secondary RDD survey analyses (Boxell et al., 2017; Holmes & McNeal, 2016).

Moving beyond correlational relationships, our 3-wave panel data are unique as it focuses specifically on social media news reading on Facebook over time and shows that social newsfeeds promote increased longitudinal exposure to counter-attitudinal sources. Our panel survey data also allow us to move beyond mere exposure and test the influence of news exposure on affective polarization. While our results showed some support for a theoretically driven depolarization process model, we must note that our panel survey results are subject to alternative explanations given the many moving parts in a campaign. It is also possible that the three-month window just prior to the election was inappropriate for finding polarization effects that happened over the course of a much longer Presidential campaign. We chose this window as it opened just after the major party candidates were officially nominated. Past research has shown that this is the most active period for campaign ad spending and political communication among voters (Fowler, Ridout, & Franz, 2016; Hardy & Scheufele, 2009). Ultimately, these findings should be replicated in different contexts and using different methods.

Another limitation of our study is that we focus specifically on Facebook use. Other social media platforms like Twitter or Weibo may present different results. We chose Facebook as our focal social media platform because it is used vastly more frequently than other SNSs for news in the US. In fact, Pew Research noted that nearly half (44%) of US adults used Facebook for news in 2016 compared to YouTube (10%), Twitter (9%), or Instagram (4%) (Gottfried & Shearer, 2016). We have argued elsewhere (Beam, Haridakis, Hutchens, & Hmielowski, 2017) that Twitter's popularity as a platform for political figures during the 2016 campaign was effective because traditional media sources amplified their online posts rather than voters actually encountering the content on the social media platform. However, future research should test our theoretical model on competing platforms as social media use evolves over time.

Conclusion

Taken as a whole, our study indicates that news on Facebook, social media filter bubbles, and echo chambers may not be the culprit for rising citizen polarization. Instead, our results indicate that Facebook news use is relatively infrequent. Despite the fact that Facebook is steadily growing in its power relative to online news audiences, traditional sources and platforms of news like cable news and interpersonal discussion remain entrenched as people's primary venues for election information (see Beam et al., 2017). Rising partisanship is problematic for democratic institutions. We also believe that growing questions of spreading misinformation and partisan fragmentation deserve additional attention.

However, our findings suggest that critiques of social and algorithmic platforms may receive greater dominance in our scholarly and journalistic discourse about democratic problems than warranted. Instead, potential alternative explanations for growing affective polarization among citizens such as elite polarization, global media system changes, money in political campaigns, or institutional changes that promote inequality should be explored.

Disclosure statement

No potential conflict of interest was reported by the authors.

Notes on contributors

Michael A. Beam, PhD (mbeam6@kent.edu) is an assistant professor in the School of Communication Studies at Kent State University. His research interests include political communication and new communication technologies.

Myiah J. Hutchens, PhD (myiah.hutchens@gmail.com) is an assistant professor in the Edward R. Murrow College of Communication at Washington State University. Her research interests include political communication and political discussion.

Jay D. Hmielowski, PhD (jay.hmielowski@gmail.com) is an assistant professor in the Edward R. Murrow College of Communication at Washington State University. His research interests include political communication and environmental communication.

ORCID

Michael A. Beam http://orcid.org/0000-0003-2425-2010

References

Abramowitz, A. I. (2010). *The disappearing center: Engaged citizens, polarization, and American democracy*. New Haven, CT: Yale University Press.

Abramowitz, A. I., & Saunders, K. L. (2008). Is polarization a myth? *The Journal of Politics, 70*(2), 542–555.

Andrejevic, M. (2013). *Infoglut: How too much information is changing the way we think and know*. New York, NY: Routledge.

Ansolabehere, S., & Rivers, D. (2013). Cooperative survey research. *Annual Review of Political Science, 16*, 307–329.

Ansolabehere, S., & Schaffner, B. F. (2014). Does survey mode still matter? Findings from a 2010 multi-mode comparison. *Political Analysis, 22*(3), 285–303.

Anspach, N. M. (2017). The new personal influence: How our Facebook friends influence the news we read. *Political Communication, 34*, 590–606.

Bakshy, E., Messing, S., & Adamic, L. A. (2015). Exposure to ideologically diverse news and opinion on Facebook. *Science, 348*, 1130–1132.

Beam, M. A. (2014). Automating the news: How personalized news recommender system design choices impact news reception. *Communication Research, 41*(8), 1019–1041.

Beam, M. A., Haridakis, P. M., Hutchens, M. J., & Hmielowski, J. (2017). Social media, news platforms, and partisan exposure: Voters' media preferences during the 2016 presidential campaign season. In D. Schill & J. Hendricks (Eds.), *The presidency and social media: Discourse, disruption, and digital democracy in the 2016 presidential election* (pp. 37–55). New York, NY: Routledge.

Beam, M. A., Hutchens, M. J., & Hmielowski, J. D. (2016). Clicking vs. sharing: The relationship between online news behaviors and political knowledge. *Computers in Human Behavior, 59*, 215–220.

Bello, J., & Rolfe, M. (2013). Is influence mightier than selection? Forging agreement in political discussion networks during a campaign. *Social Networks, 36*, 134–146.

Benkler, Y., Faris, R., Roberts, H., & Zuckerman, E. (2017, March 3). Study: Breitbart-led right-wing media ecosystem altered broader media agenda. *Columbia Journalism Review*. Retrieved from https://www.cjr.org/analysis/breitbart-media-trump-harvard-study.php

Boxell, L., Gentzkow, M., & Shapiro, J. M. (2017). Greater Internet use is not associated with faster growth in political polarization among US demographic groups. *PNAS, 114*, 10612–10617.

Delli Carpini, M. X., & Keeter, S. (1996). *What Americans know about politics and why it matters*. New Haven, CT: Yale University Press.

Donsbach, W., & Mothes, C. (2012). The dissonant self: Contributions from dissonance theory to a new agenda for studying political communication. In C. T. Salmon (Ed.), *Communication yearbook 36* (pp. 3–44). New York: Taylor & Francis.

Dylko, I., Dolgov, I., Hoffman, W., Eckhart, N., Molina, M., & Aaziz, O. (2018). Impact of customizability technology on political polarization. *Journal of Information Technology & Politics, 15*, 19–33.

Fiorina, M., Abrams, S., & Pope, J. (2011). *Culture war?: The myth of a polarized America*. New York, NY: Pearson Longman.

Flaxman, S., Goel, S., & Rao, J. M. (2016). Filter bubbles, echo chambers, and online news consumption. *Public Opinion Quarterly, 80*(S1), 298–320.

Fowler, E. F., Ridout, T. N., & Franz, M. M. (2016). Political advertising in 2016: The presidential election as outlier? *The Forum, 14*(4), 445–469.

Garrett, R. K. (2009). Politically motivated reinforcement seeking: Reframing the selective exposure debate. *Journal of Communication, 59*, 676–699.

Garrett, R. K., Carnahan, D., & Lynch, E. K. (2013). A turn toward avoidance? Selective exposure to online political information, 2004–2008. *Political Behavior, 35*(1), 113–134.

Garrett, R. K., Dvir-Gvirsman, S., Johnson, B. K., Tsfati, Y., Neo, R., & Dal, A. (2014). Implications of pro- and counterattitudinal information exposure for affective polarization. *Human Communication Research, 40*(3), 309–332.

Garrett, R. K., & Stroud, N. J. (2014). Partisan oaths to exposure diversity: Differences in pro-and counterattitudinal news consumption. *Journal of Communication, 64*(4), 680–701.

Gentzkow, M., & Shapiro, J. M. (2011). Ideological segregation online and offline. *Quarterly Journal of Economics, 126*(4), 1799–1839.

Gil de Zúñiga, H., Weeks, B., & Ardèvol-Abreu, A. (2017). Effects of the news-finds-me perception in communication: Social media use implications for news seeking and learning about politics. *Journal of Computer-Mediated Communication, 22*(3), 105–123.

Gottfried, J., & Shearer, E. (2016, May 26). *News use across social media platforms 2016*. Retrieved from http://www.journalism.org/2016/05/26/news-use-across-social-media-platforms-2016/

Hardy, B. W., & Scheufele, D. A. (2009). Presidential campaign dynamics and the ebb and flow of talk as a moderator: Media exposure, knowledge, and political discussion. *Communication Theory, 19*(1), 89–101.

Hmielowski, J. D. (2012). Intramedia moderation, electoral ambivalence, and electoral decision making. *Mass Communication and Society, 15*(3), 454–477.

Hmielowski, J. D., Beam, M. A., & Hutchens, M. J. (2016). Structural changes in media and attitude polarization: Examining the contributions of TV news before and after the Telecommunications Act of 1996. *International Journal of Public Opinion Research, 18*(2), 123–143.

Hmielowski, J. D., Beam, M. A., & Hutchens, M. J. (2017). Bridging the partisan divide? Exploring ambivalence and information seeking over time in the 2012 US presidential election. *Mass Communication and Society, 20*(3), 336–357.

Holmes, J. W., & McNeal, R. S. (2016). Social media, participation, and attitudes: Does social media drive polarization? In T. Deželan & I. Vobič (Eds.), *(R)evolutionizing political communication through social media* (pp. 1–21). Hershey, PA: Information Science Reference.

Iyengar, S., Sood, G., & Lelkes, Y. (2012). Affect, not ideology: A social identity perspective on polarization. *Public Opinion Quarterly*, *76*(3), 405–421.

Kim, Y. (2015). Does disagreement mitigate polarization? How selective exposure and disagreement affect political polarization. *Journalism & Mass Communication Quarterly*, *92*(4), 915–937.

Lawrence, E., Sides, J., & Farrell, H. (2010). Self-segregation or deliberation? Blog relationships, participation, and polarization in American politics. *Perspectives in Politics*, *8*, 141–157.

Lelkes, Y., Sood, G., & Iyengar, S. (2017). The hostile audience: The effect of access to broadband internet on partisan affect. *American Journal of Political Science*, *61*(1), 5–20.

Lessig, L. (2011). *Republic, lost: How money corrupts congress – and a plan to stop it*. New York, NY: Twelve.

McCarty, N., Poole, K. T., & Rosenthal, H. (2016). *Polarized America: The dance of ideology and unequal riches* (2nd ed.). Cambridge, MA: MIT Press.

Messing, S., & Westwood, S. J. (2014). Selective exposure in the age of social media: Endorsements trump partisan source affiliation when selecting news online. *Communication Research*, *41*(8), 1042–1063.

Mutz, D. C. (2006). *Hearing the other side: Deliberative versus participatory democracy*. New York, NY: Cambridge University Press.

Pariser, E. (2011). *The filter bubble: What the Internet is hiding from you*. New York: Penguin.

Pek, J., & Hoyle, R. H. (2016). On the (in)validity of tests of simple mediation: Threats and solutions. *Social and Personality Psychology Compass*, *10*(3), 150–163.

Prior, M. (2007). *Post-broadcast democracy: How media choice increases inequality in political involvement and polarizes elections*. Cambridge, UK: Cambridge University Press.

Prior, M. (2013). Media and political polarization. *Annual Review of Political Science*, *16*, 101–127.

Slater, M. D. (2007). Reinforcing spirals: The mutual influence of media selectivity and media effects and their impact on individual behavior and social identity. *Communication Theory*, *17* (3), 281–303.

Slater, M. D. (2015). Reinforcing spirals model: Conceptualizing the relationship between media content exposure and the development and maintenance of attitudes. *Media Psychology*, *18*(3), 370–395.

Stroud, N. J. (2014). Selective exposure theories. In K. Kenski & K. H. Jamieson (Eds.), *Oxford Handbook of Political Communication*. New York: Oxford University Press. doi:10.1093/oxfordhb/9780199793471.013.009

Sunstein, C. R. (2017). *#Republic: Divided democracy in the age of social media*. Princeton, NJ: Princeton University Press.

Tufekci, Z. (2015). Facebook said its algorithms do help form echo chambers, and the tech press missed it. *New Perspectives Quarterly*, *32*(3), 9–12.

US Census Bureau. (2016). American Fact Finder. Retrieved from https://factfinder.census.gov.

Weeks, B. E., & Holbert, R. L. (2013). Predicting dissemination of news content in social media: A focus on reception, friending, and partisanship. *Journalism and Mass Communication Quarterly*, *90*(2), 212–232.

Weeks, B. E., Lane, D. S., Kim, D. H., Lee, S. S., & Kwak, N. (2017). Incidental exposure, selective exposure, and political information sharing: Integrating online exposure patterns and expression on social media. *Journal of Computed Mediated Communication*, *22*, 363–379.

Yamamoto, M., Kushin, M. J., & Dalisay, F. (2015). Social media and mobiles as political mobilization forces for young adults: Examining the moderating role of online political expression in political participation. *New Media & Society*, *17*, 880–898.

Appendix

Table A1. Survey demographic and US demographic summaries.

Variable	Survey[a]	US Census[b]
Sex: Female[c]	51.5%	51.6%[f]
Age	46.70[e]	45–54[d,f]
Hispanic[c]	16.0%	17.3%
Race: White[c]	77.8%	76%
Race: African-American/Black[c]	12.8%	13.8%
Race: Asian American/Asian[c]	3.4%	6.2%
Race: Native American[c]	2.2%	1.7%
Race: Other[c]	7.4%	5.7%
Education[d]	Some College	Some College
Income[d]	50-under 75k	$55,322

Notes: [a]$N = 500$, [b]Source: 2012–2016 American Community Survey (US Census Bureau, 2016), [c]Proportion, [d]Median, [e]Mean, and [f]US population over 18.

Table A2. Facebook estimates of lagged analysis of Facebook news use and affective polarization.

	Facebook News Use		
	Wave 1	Wave 2	Wave 3
Wave 1 Facebook	–	.729 (.678–.777)*	–
Wave 2 Facebook	–	–	.685 (.621–.746)*
Wave 3 Facebook	–	–	–
Wave 1 Polarization	6.95 (2.439–11.645)*	−.005 (−.008– −.002)*	–
Wave 2 Polarization	–	−.012 (−1.969–1.897)	.000 (−.004–.003)
Wave 3 Polarization	–	–	.430 (−1.851–2.810)
Gender	.367 (.061–.654)*	–	–
Income	−.067 (−.139–.007)	–	–
Education	−.049 (−.134–.037)	–	–
Age	−.017 (−.025– −.009)*	–	–
White	−.168 (−.466–.134)	–	–
Ideology	.099 (.009–.186)*	–	–
Political Interest	.275 (.188–.360)*	–	–
R^2	.109	.566	.501

Note: Cell entries are unstandardized coefficients with 95% CI in parentheses. *indicates that the 95% CI does not cover zero.

Table A3. Affective polarization estimates of lagged analysis of Facebook news use and affective polarization.

	Affective Polarization		
	Wave 1	Wave 2	Wave 3
Wave 1 Facebook	6.95 (2.439–11.645)*	−.379 (.−1.474–.771)	
Wave 2 Facebook		−.012(−1.969–1.897)	−1.27 (−2.534– −.036)*
Wave 3 Facebook			.430 (−1.851–2.810)
Wave 1 Polarization		.767 (.707–.821)*	
Wave 2 Polarization			.730 (.661–.791)*
Wave 3 Polarization			
Gender	1.547 (−4.343–7.070)		
Income	.228 (−1.220–1.660)		
Education	.635 (−1.071–2.321)		
Age	.298 (.142–.460)*		
White	1.098 (−5.120–7.648)		
Ideology	1.278 (−.544–2.964)		
Political interest	3.970 (1.931–5.913)*		
R^2	.086	.595	.545

Note: Cell entries are unstandardized coefficients with 95% CI in parentheses. * indicates that the 95% CI does not cover zero.

Table A4. Facebook estimates for lagged analysis of Facebook news use, pro- and counter-attitudinal exposure, and affective polarization.

	Facebook news use		
	Wave 1	Wave 2	Wave 3
Wave 1 Facebook	–	.688 (.635–.745)	–
Wave 2 Facebook	–	–	.661 (.598–.725)*
Wave 3 Facebook	–	–	–
Wave 1 Polarization	6.877 (1.922–11.062)*	−.005 (−.008 – −.002)*	–
Wave 2 Polarization	–	−.004 (−1.989–1.895)	.000 (−.004–.004)
Wave 3 Polarization	–	–	.685 (−1.531–3.112)
Wave 1 Counter	.367 (.230–.525)*	.096 (−.005–.186)	–
Wave 2 Counter	–	.367 (.230–.525)*	.060 (−.051–.181)
Wave 3 Counter	–	–	.367 (.003–.200)*
Wave 1 Pro	.552 (.368–.725)*	.079 (.004–.159)*	–
Wave 2 Pro	–	.178 (.096–.276)*	.050 (−.033–.132)
Wave 3 Pro	–	–	.271 (.172–.382)*
Gender	.367 (.077–.672)*	–	–
Income	.023 (−.028–.072)	–	–
Education	.008 (−.044–.064)	–	–
Age	−.014 (−.019 – −.009)*	–	–
White	−.168 (−.488–.116)	–	–
Ideology	.099 (.008–.192)*	–	–
Political Interest	.275 (.184–.362)*	–	–
R^2	.109	.577	.505

Note: Cell entries are unstandardized coefficients with 95% CI in parentheses. * indicates that the 95% CI does not cover zero.

Table A5. Affective polarization estimates for lagged analysis of Facebook news use, pro- and counter-attitudinal exposure, and affective polarization

	Affective Polarization		
	Wave 1	Wave 2	Wave 3
Wave 1 Facebook	6.877 (1.922–11.062)*	−.277 (−1.500–1.011)	–
Wave 2 Facebook	–	−.004 (−1.989–1.895)	−.630 (−1.936–.866)
Wave 3 Facebook	–	–	.685 (−1.531–3.112)
Wave 1 Polarization	–	.754 (.692–.813)*	–
Wave 2 Polarization	–	–	.710 (.635–.782)*
Wave 3 Polarization	–	–	–
Wave 1 Counter	−4.901 (−7.835– −2.434)*	−1.391 (−3.416–.486)	–
Wave 2 Counter	–	−.607 (−2.388–1.178)	−2.390 (−5.19 – −.231)*
Wave 3 Counter	–	–	−.728 (−2.225–.619)
Wave 1 Pro	.600 (−3.434–4.141)	.773 (−.769–2.209)	–
Wave 2 Pro	–	1.933 (−.020–4.306)	−.654 (−2.570–1.032)
Wave 3 Pro	–	–	2.835 (.696–5.156)*
Gender	1.430 (−4.631–7.048)	–	–
Income	.288 (−1.139–1.759)	–	–
Education	.667 (−.963–2.299)	–	–
Age	2.93 (.131–.455)*	–	–
White	.795 (−5.488–7.514)	–	–
Ideology	1.162 (−.584–2.931)	–	–
Political interest	3.880 (1.923–5.770)*	–	–
R^2	.084	.599	.555

Note: Cell entries are unstandardized coefficients with 95% CI in parentheses. * indicates 95% CI does not cover zero

Table A6. Counter-attitudinal exposure estimates for lagged analysis of Facebook news use, pro- and counter-attitudinal exposure, and affective polarization.

	Counter-Attitudinal Exposure		
	Wave 1	Wave 2	Wave 3
Wave 1 Facebook	.367 (.230–.525)*	.043 (−.006 – .099)	–
Wave 2 Facebook	–	.094 (.006–.186)*	.083 (.037–.135)*
Wave 3 Facebook	–	–	.095 (.003–.200)*
Wave 1 Polarization	−4.901 (−7.835– .2.434)*	−.008 (−.012 – −.006)*	–
Wave 2 Polarization	–	−.607 (−2.388–.1.178)	−.003 (−.006 – −.001)*
Wave 3 Polarization	–	–	−.728 (−2.225–.619)
Wave 1 Counter	–	.511 (.404–.621)	–
Wave 2 Counter	–	–	.612 (.524–.708)*
Wave 3 Counter	–	–	–
Wave 1 Pro	.532 (.421–.667)*	–	–
Wave 2 Pro	–	.387 (.276–.500)*	–
Wave 3 Pro	–	–	.259 (.183–.360)*
Gender	.048 (−.117–.232)	–	–
Income	.023 (−.028–.072)	–	–
Education	.008 (−.044–.064)	–	–
Age	−.014 (−.019 – −.009)*	–	–
White	−.736 (−.982 – −.536)*	–	–
Ideology	.019 (−.041 – .079)	–	–
Political interest	.101 (.048 – .162)*	–	–
R^2	.189	.377	.514

Note: Cell entries are unstandardized coefficients with 95% CI in parentheses. * indicates 95% CI does not cover zero

Table A7. Pro-attitudinal exposure estimates for lagged analysis of Facebook news use, pro- and counter-attitudinal exposure, and affective polarization.

	Pro-attitudinal exposure		
	Wave 1	Wave 2	Wave 3
Wave 1 Facebook	.552 (.368–.762)*	.005 (−.049–.060)	–
Wave 2 Facebook	–	.178 (.096–.276)*	.054 (−.002–.118)
Wave 3 Facebook	–	–	.271 (.172–.382)*
Wave 1 Polarization	.600 (−3.434–4.141)	−.001 (−.004–.002)	–
Wave 2 Polarization	–	1.933 (−.020–4.306)	.001 (−.002–.004)
Wave 3 Polarization	–	–	2.835 (.696–5.156)*
Wave 1 Counter	.532 (.421–.667)*	–	–
Wave 2 Counter	–	.387 (.276–.500)*	–
Wave 3 Counter	–	–	.259 (.183–.360)*
Wave 1 Pro	–	.723 (.657–.782)*	–
Wave 2 Pro	–	–	.781 (.711–.840)*
Wave 3 Pro	–	–	–
Gender	−.253 (−.491 – −.017)*	–	–
Income	.070 (.007–.127)*	–	–
Education	.013 (−.052–.075)	–	–
Age	.005 (−.002–.011)	–	–
White	−.340 (−.615 – −.104)*	–	–
Ideology	.074 (.000–.148)*	–	–
Political Interest	.352 (.273–.424)*	–	–
R^2	.243	.558	.581

Note: Cell entries are unstandardized coefficients with 95% CI in parentheses. * indicates 95% CI does not cover zero

OPEN ACCESS

3 Do not blame it on the algorithm

An empirical assessment of multiple recommender systems and their impact on content diversity

Judith Möller, Damian Trilling, Natali Helberger and Bram van Es

ABSTRACT

In the debate about filter bubbles caused by algorithmic news recommendation, the conceptualization of the two core concepts in this debate, diversity and algorithms, has received little attention in social scientific research. This paper examines the effect of multiple recommender systems on different diversity dimensions. To this end, it maps different values that diversity can serve, and a respective set of criteria that characterizes a diverse information offer in this particular conception of diversity. We make use of a data set of simulated article recommendations based on actual content of one of the major Dutch broadsheet newspapers and its users (*N*=21,973 articles, *N*=500 users). We find that all of the recommendation logics under study proved to lead to a rather diverse set of recommendations that are on par with human editors and that basing recommendations on user histories can substantially increase topic diversity within a recommendation set.

1. Introduction

Functioning democracies rely on the media's role to enable different groups and interests in society to participate in the democratic debate and create the opportunity for citizens to encounter diverse opinions (Owen & Smith, 2015). Therefore, diversity is one of the core public values in media law and policy. As the Council of Europe (2007) has put it, 'media pluralism and diversity of media content are essential for the functioning of a democratic society' and the right to freedom of expression 'will be fully satisfied only if each person is given the possibility to form his or her own opinion from diverse sources of information'. The close link between media diversity and democratic participation may also explain the vigor with which new technological innovations in the media landscape are being met. The impact of personalized recommendations and algorithmic filtering on users' information diet is subject to dystopian visions about filter bubbles and echo chambers. But how much

CONTACT Judith Möller j.e.moller1@uva.nl

reason do we actually have to be concerned about the diversity of algorithmic recommendations?

The aim of the present study is to better understand the effect of different recommender systems on diversity. We will do so in the form of a data-scientific experiment, in which we compare simulated recommendation sets with regard to their performance on several indicators of diversity to human editors.

Scholars of selective exposure have often argued that once given enough choice, users voluntarily lock themselves up in so-called 'echo chambers', in which they are only exposed to like-minded content (e.g. Stroud, 2011). Recently, this line of reasoning has been extended: Pariser (2011) argues that algorithmic selections contribute to a situation in which users are essentially exposed to a self-confirming feedback loop. He described the resulting spaces with like-minded information as 'filter bubbles'. That has raised concerns that societies will become increasingly polarized and fragmented. However, given that the diversity of news selected by human editors is also constrained on the individual, organizational, and structural level (Shoemaker et al., 2001) and that users play a very active role users in selecting and processing news, this line of reasoning attributes more power to algorithmic news recommendation services than they probably deserve (Zuiderveen Borgesius et al., 2016). First empirical studies indicate that, at present, algorithmic recommendation systems have not locked large segments of the audience into bubbles (Fletcher & Nielsen, 2017).

Moreover, an important lacuna in the current debate about potential filter bubbles is the lack of attention for two core concepts, *diversity* and *algorithmic selection*. So far, diversity is mainly discussed and measured in terms of political leaning of news sources and stories (e.g. Flaxman & Rao, 2016), thereby neglecting that diversity is a multi-dimensional concept that also encompasses topic plurality, genre, or the plurality in tone (Helberger et al., 2018). It is also often assumed that the appropriate level of analysis is the bubble of content created by one outlet. There has been little research so far that would translate the very relevant body of research on exposure diversity (Napoli, 2015) into measures that can be used to assess the performance of algorithmic recommender systems.

This study contributes to the current body of work on the effect of algorithmic news personalization on exposure diversity in three ways. We start out with proposing a first set of concrete indicators that can help us to assess the diversity of different recommendation algorithms. Second, we study the consequences of different algorithmic design choices in depth. In the current debate, news recommendation algorithms are often treated as a single entity and considered to be an immutable, external force. That is, however, a misrepresentation of reality. While it may be true that some or even many of the current recommender algorithms are optimized predominantly on short-term metrics such as clicks, a whole range of recommendation algorithms are available and used. In order to understand the effects of a recommendation algorithm on individual's news diet, it is important to understand that potential effects of recommendation algorithms are dependent on the exact design of the recommendation algorithm in use (see also Kitchin, 2017). The third and main contribution is the development of a new and innovative method we use to measure diversity in news recommendation sets. It goes beyond existing methods that assess diversity by classifying content as either falling in the same category (not diverse) or not falling in the same category (diverse). By taking into account that many of the categories are related to one another, we can measure the complexity of diversity in news more accurately. For example, a story about international relations has arguably a different topic than a story about national politics, yet, compared to a story about biology they are quite similar. In order to fully assess how diverse recommendation sets are we need to include this notion of *relative* distance to our model. Finally, we use two benchmarks to evaluate the performance of the recommender systems against in terms of diversity. The first is empirical and represents the selection of news articles by human editors. The second is statistical and assumes a completely random selection over all articles.

2. Dissecting diversity

As the phenomenon of algorithmic news recommendation is still recent and constantly in development, there are few empirical studies on potentially lacking diversity of news recommendation systems in the field of social science (for an overview, see Dylko et al., 2017). The first set of studies (Dylko et al., 2017; Beam, 2014; O'Callaghan et al., 2015; Bakshy et al., 2015) have coherently provided evidence that unobtrusive and automatic selection of content can reduce exposure diversity in the context of news. However, whether that is the case or not depends on the exact settings of the algorithmic recommendation system and the data that is used to determine the recommendations as research in the field of informatics and data science has demonstrated. In fact, algorithmic design can also increase diversity (Smyth & McClave, 2001). Moreover, studies combining insights form the field of computer science with psychology have repeatedly shown that diversity in recommendation sets increases user satisfaction (Knijnenburg et al., 2012; Ziegler et al., 2005; Willemsen et al., 2016). According to this strand of literature, diverse recommendations have a distinct function in the selection decision process. They support the user in the exploratory stage of interaction with the recommender system to identify relevant items quicker (see also Bridge & Kelly, 2006).

The different results regarding diverse outcomes of news recommendation systems in social science and computer science are partially a consequence of different conceptualizations of diversity. Whereas diversity in the social scientific debate is often conceptualized as inclusion of counter-attitudinal information (Pariser, 2011), in computer science it is considered a necessary design element, often conceptualized as the inclusion of unexpected items. Diversity is mostly modeled and conceptualized at the input level in computer science, whereas social scientists analyze diversity primarily at the output level: Whereas the former study how to optimize the inclusion of surprising or unexpected items, social scientists focus on the overall output of a recommender system and assess its diversity (Sørensen & Schmidt, 2016).

2.1. Algorithmic design

The task of algorithms in the context of news recommendation systems is to structure and order the pool of available news according to predetermined principles. Yet, algorithms are created by humans and their design choices regarding the sorting and ranking of items influence the output (Bozdag, 2013). Three common approaches are:

(1) General popularity of the item among all users. This is the most simple approach, as all users get the same recommendation, leading to a Matthew effect, in which popular items become even more popular and unpopular items disappear.

(2) Semantic filtering. This approach recommends items that match the currently used item or items previously used by the same user on a number of pre-defined criteria (features). In the case of news articles, these features could be words or topics, but also the author or source of an article.
(3) Collaborative filtering or social information filtering. This process 'automates the process of 'word-of-mouth' recommendations: items are recommended to a user based upon values assigned by other people with similar taste' (Bozdag, 2013).

These methods are usually applied in hybrid forms, also including other methods like weighing items by recency or pushing content that has specific features (e.g. paid content). Of course, one can conceive of other structuring principles as well: A recommender system might inject an 'editor's pick' or even some random articles. A simple algorithm might offer the same results for each reader of a given article (item-to-item recommendation). More sophisticated algorithms do not only combine several of the logics mentioned above, but also take into account past user behavior and choices. That means that instead of finding the best match merely based on the article that is currently displayed, these algorithms select articles that resemble the spectrum of all articles that user has read before. When implemented properly, this can lead to a truly personalized news recommendation, implying that every reader of an article could be recommended a unique set of news items (Ricci et al., 2011). This personal profile based on past behavior can be additionally enriched by known user data such as age or location.

2.2. Diversity in algorithmic design

In addition to these logics, many recommendation systems also include an element of surprise: serendipity. Some authors even state that serendipity is a crucial element of all algorithmic recommendation systems (Kotkov et al., 2016). Serendipitous recommenders do not select all items they present to users according to the principles presented above. Some items are included at random. This serves two purposes: First, the chance that users lose interest because the choice set is too uniform decreases. Second, these items are needed for algorithms to learn and improve themselves. Consider the example of a user starting to use a recommendation system during a soccer world championship. Chances are high that this person will read a couple of sports articles in a row – maybe even nothing else. If an aggressively personalized recommendation system would now recommend *only* sports articles in the upcoming week, the user would not only get frustrated, but the system would have no chance of learning that the user is actually much more interested in economics than in sport. Serendipity is also needed to integrate *new* items into a recommendation system: For new articles, information about who read it is simply not available.

In computer science, there is no consensus on how serendipity should be conceptualized and operationalized, other than unexpectedness (Kotkov et al., 2016). Serendipity is not fully synonymous with diversity in this strand of literature. While both serendipity and diversity describe the relationship between user and item, diversity specifically describes the differences in content. It is usually measured as an overlap between content features (see Kunaver & Požrl, 2017). Many users appreciate diversity in the realm of news, but a key challenge is finding a balance between accuracy of the recommendation and diversity of the recommendation set (see, e.g. Ribeiro et al., 2015).

2.3. Diversity in the social sciences

In the social-scientific debate about the effects of algorithmic news recommendation on diversity, diversity is often conceptualized as ideologically cross-cutting exposure. For instance, Dylko (2016) examined the effects of user-driven versus system-driven customizable recommendation technology, and found that exposure to system-driven recommendation technology can result in political selective exposure, especially when combined with ideology-based customizability. They regard diversity as a form of selective exposure, as defined as 'proportionally high levels of consumption of information that supports one's political beliefs or attitudes, and proportionally low levels of consumption of information that is counter to one's political beliefs or attitudes' (p. 393). Beam (2014) measured diversity in terms of exposure to headlines from counter-attitudinal sources. O'Callaghan et al. (2015) showed that the YouTube recommendation system is likely to recommend extreme right-wing content if a user has just watched an extreme right-wing video. A study into Facebook's algorithmically ranked news-feed again measured diversity in the sense of 'exposure to ideologically cross cutting content' (Bakshy et al., 2015). In contrast, Haim et al. (2017) focused on source and content diversity, whereby they measured content diversity in terms of categories and source diversity in terms of percentage of articles per news outlet.

In short, most studies measure exposure diversity in the context of news personalization in terms of exposure to counter-attitudinal or counter-ideological content. This is relatively straightforward, but also rather limited. While this is a fruitful approach to study polarization in bipartisan regimes, it neglects other facets of diversity that are instrumental to especially multi-party systems (see also Benson, 2009).

In reality, news content diversity is a far richer, and far more complex phenomenon (see, e.g. Helberger et al., 2018; Sørensen & Schmidt, 2016; Masini et al., 2017; Napoli, 2015). As Van Cuilenburg (1999) puts it, diversity defines the 'heterogeneity of media content in terms of one or more specified characteristics' (p. 188). In the context of media policy, diversity is often defined and measured as diversity of sources in a media market (e.g. The Media Pluralism Monitor in Europe or the FTC's controversial Diversity Index; Napoli, 2015; Karppinen, 2013). However, for the purpose of measuring the diversity of personalized recommendations, source-centered approaches to measuring media diversity are only of little help, particularly in the European context where press self-regulation emphasizes *internal* diversity of (quality) news media. They can already been criticized on a more theoretical, normative basis. Duncan & Reid (2013) warn that they 'emphasize diversity for diversity's sake, leading to a postmodern, relativistic "anything goes" approach to public discourse, where society's most pressing concerns are drowned in a cacophony of different voices' (p. 486). More practically, most of the existing approaches look at media markets in their entirety (external diversity) (Karppinen, 2015), and less at the diversity within a particular outlet (internal diversity). Obviously, assessing the diversity of the results of personalized recommendations requires an assessment at the (internal) level of the recommendation, or respectively the output of a personalized recommendation[1].

2.4. Diversity as a function of news in democracy

But what is then a diverse recommendation set? The answer depends on what information users need in order to be able to fulfill their role in a specific model of democracy (e.g. Strömbäck, 2005; Ferree et al., 2002): Different theories of democracy (e.g. procedural, competitive, participatory, or deliberative) imply different communication needs (e.g. marketplace of ideas, creation of understanding and tolerance, or opportunity to explore news autonomously). Ideally, these different conceptualizations should be taken into account before making any claims about the impact of algorithmic filtering on the state of the democratic debate. Hence, there can be different types of diversity standing next to each other. Some maybe more suitable for personalized recommendations in the public service media, others in the commercial media, local or regional outlets, etc.

One essential characteristic of algorithmic recommendations is a user interest-driven approach: based on the different *interests* of users that an algorithmic recommender infers, it makes recommendations. This user interest-driven and topics-centered approach also reflects the move towards disintegration and decentralization of news, which is not at least a result of new, algorithmically driven media platforms, be that media services such as *Upday* or *Flipboard*, or more general purpose platforms, such as social networks and search engines. They might serve people 'more of the same' (e.g. Sunstein, 2007) and fail to represent the diversity of topics in society. This is why one dimension of the diversity that we will look at is the diversity of topics.

In a participatory model of democracy, in which the task of the media is to inform citizens in a way that allows them to actively participate in politics, exposure diversity also depends on the ratio of politically relevant content. A democratically responsible recommender from this perspective would ensure that important political topics for the public agenda reach the user. In contrast, from the perspective of a more procedural concept of exposure diversity, the ability to participate actively in politics is less prominent, whereas the importance of fundamental rights, such as freedom of expression, privacy and informational self-determination come to the fore. From this perspective, the outcome of diverse recommendation logics can be compared to what extent we can observe differences between personalized and non-personalized recommendation settings, or, in other words, how well the recommender performs in individualizing the information offer based on the signals from the user.

From a deliberative democracy point of view, not only the topics represented, but also the tone in which they are presented matters. Since the ultimate goal is (rational and fair) deliberation, this should also be reflected in the tone in which topics are represented: measured, informative, reconcillary, and non-aggressive. In contrast, under a more participative conception of exposure diversity, where diversity serves as a means to inform, enable and activate citizens to play a more active role in society, arguably, the tone can at times also veer into the direction of activist, engaging, critical and even partial and one-sided. Critical can also be the tone in a more competitive conceptualization of exposure diversity, where citizens are expected to be informed about current and future societal problems and who is the best able to solve them; but less than in a participatory model, those do not need to be sweeping, activating statements. A matter-of-fact to critical tone in describing the issues would seem more conductive to the goals under this particular conception of exposure diversity.

3. Method

We present a first attempt of an empirical assessment of recommender diversity based on the considerations outlined above. It should be noted that we are explicitly not researching viewpoint diversity. As we are using a most similar experimental design, we rely on a set of articles and recommendations from one newspaper, which limits the possibilities to study ideological diversity or diversity in style. The focus of this study is, as outlined above, topics (both in general, as the 'politicalness' of the topics). Taking these as examples, we show how to construct a multi-dimensional feature space that allows us to assess the diversity of recommendation sets. We then evaluate how different recommender systems perform on these criteria.

3.1. Research design

To study the influence of algorithmic design on diversity, we carry out a data-scientific experiment. Specifically, we compare the output of different algorithmic news recommendation for the same articles of the same news source (*de Volkskrant*, a Dutch progressive high-quality newspaper, that is oriented towards the political center, see Figure 1). Our dataset also includes recommendation sets for each of the articles that have been picked by human editors. This provides us with a unique benchmark to evaluate the performance of the recommender systems.

For *N*=1000 articles that were published between 19–9–2016 and 26–9–2016, we simulated which three articles out of the pool of *N*=21,973 articles would be recommended if one of the following logics were used:

(1) The choice of human editors
(2) The overall popularity

Figure 1. Recommendation box on the newspaper website. The recommendation box is displayed in the top right corner ('Aanbevolen artikelen').

(3) Collaborative filtering (item-to-item)
(4) Semantic filtering (item-to-item)
(5) Collaborative filtering (taking into account user histories)
(6) Semantic filtering (taking into account user histories)
(7) A random baseline, in which each article is equally likely to be recommended.

For the two algorithms that are based on user histories, we used the tracking history of 500 randomly selected news users.

3.2. Feature engineering

As the dataset contained rich information on each article (e.g. not only the full text, but also a category label and topic tags), we could create multiple sets of features.

3.2.1. Topic distance

We used the package Gensim (Řehůřek & Sojka, 2010) to estimate a topic model. After evaluating different models based on their perplexity and interpretability, we chose an LDA model (Blei et al., 2003) with 50 topics based on $tf \cdot idf$ representations of the documents, with additional filtering of extremely common and extremely uncommon words. We used pyLDAvis (see Sievert & Shirley, 2014) to perform multidimensional scaling on the resulting topics. As a result, each topic can be represented by its coordinates (x,y) in a two-dimensional space. As the Euclidian distance between two points is $\sqrt{(x_2 - x_1)^2 + (y_2 - y_1)^2}$, and as each document D is represented by a vector $\vec{w_D}$ of 50 topic weights $w_{D,1} \cdots w_{D,50}$, we can calculate the topic distance between two documents.[2]

3.2.2. Category and tag distance

Another more recent approach is the use of word embeddings to capture the aggregate inter-document difference, basically by considering the Wasserstein metric describing the minimum effort to make two documents similar. This is called the word mover distance (WMD). The great benefit of this method is that it is not sensitive to non-overlapping document vocabularies. We use a word vector model pre-trained on the NLCOW14 corpus (see Tulkens et al., 2016; Schäfer & Bildhauer, 2012), which we again apply using Gensim.

In addition, we also have human-labeled tags as proxies for the topics and we have the newspaper sections for each article as proxies for the categories. We again apply the word-distance derived from the word vector trained on the NLCOW14 corpus.

3.2.3. Ratio of politically relevant content

To estimate the topical distance from politics and related terms, we first construct a list of 20 words that are closest to 'politiek' (politics/political) according to our word vector model, plus a manual selection. This list of words is then compared with the words in the article text.

3.2.4. Tone distance

We estimated the polarity and subjectivity of the articles using the package Pattern (De Smedt & Daelemans, 2012). Pattern has been used before to estimate the sentiment of

Dutch-language newspaper coverage (Junqué de Fortuny et al., 2012). For each article, it returns a tuple with two values: the polarity, ranging from negative (−1) to positive (+1), and the subjectivity, ranging from a very objective tone (0) to a very subjective one (+1). Using these tuples as coordinates, we can situate each article in a two-dimensional sentiment space.

3.3. Diversity evaluation

Having obtained the pairwise distances, we will describe their distributions per recommender system.

Additionally, we can apply formal diversity measures such as Rao's quadratic entropy/diversity (see Ricotta & Szeidl, 2006). It was originally intended to reflect biodiversity and is given by the following equation

$$\begin{aligned}\mathcal{H}_{Rao,entropy} &= \sum\sum p_i p_j d_{i,j} \\ \mathcal{H}_{Rao,diversity} &= \sum_{j=1} p_j \sum_{i \neq j} d_{i,j} p_i\end{aligned} \tag{1}$$

where p_i,p_j represent the proportion of a species i or j respectively and $d_{i,j}$ is some distance metric. For the present paper, the species is a reflection of document categories and the distance metric is given by the similarity between the feature vectors of the document pairs.

We calculate Rao's quadratic entropy based on the main section titles, as they are readily available and unambiguous for the distance we use, which is the cosine similarity of the word vectors for these section titles. As we are interested in diversity, not from the perspective of maintainable diverse species but rather from the perspective of a diverse representation of available categories we replace the proportions p_i and p_j by $(1 - p_i)^n$ and $(1 - p_j)^n$ respectively to create slightly adapted diversity measures. This ensures that the inclusion of niche categories contribute the most to the final diversity. In the standard formulation categories with larger proportions contribute more to the diversity.

We additionally report the Shannon entropy,

$$H_{Shannon} = -\sum p_i \log_b(p_i), \tag{2}$$

in which the relative distance between the articles is not included.

It is important to note that both Rao's quadratic entropy and Shannon's entropy will give high indications of diversity even if small niche categories are severely underrepresented or even omitted.

4. Results

Given that for each document in the dataset we simulated three recommendations (see also Figure 1), the diversity of a recommender system can be conceptualized in different ways:

(1) on the level of the recommendation set, as the mean of the distances of each article towards the original article;

(2) on the level of the recommendation set, as the mean of the distances within the recommendation set;
(3) on the user level, as the diversity of the sets of all articles a user has ever been recommended;
(4) on the level of the individual recommendation.

While all of these conceptualizations can offer valuable insights, we chose to present the results of the last conceptualization, because it avoids averaging and aggregating. As we have N=1000 origin articles ×3 recommendations, all following calculations are therefore based on N=3000 'origin article'—'recommended article' pairs.

We start by looking at the descriptive statistics of the performance of the different recommender systems. As Table 1 shows, first and foremost, differences between all systems seem to be rather limited in size. Across different operationalizations and analyses, all of the recommendation logics under study proved to lead to a rather diverse set of recommendations.

We can identify some notable tendencies, though. First of all, as one would expect, the random recommender produces one of the most diverse recommendation sets. We also see that the recommendations produced by the editors are not particularly diverse. Especially if we look at the category, we see that editors tend to recommend articles from the same or very similar categories. The results with regard to topic diversity in the output of collaborative filtering are particularly interesting. If data on past user preferences are not taken into account, collaborative filtering produces the least amount of diversity. That means if the decision which articles to show is based on the selection of other readers of the same article, it is likely that articles of the same topic are presented. Yet, if users are matched on all articles they have read, we find collaborative recommendation systems are least likely to recommend a related topic. We can conclude that in terms of topic diversity, tailoring can support diverse exposure, at least in the short run.

However, the descriptive statistics in Table 1 might hide more subtle differences. For instance, it might be the case that a recommender sometimes outputs very diverse recommendations, and sometimes recommendations that are not diverse at all, which might cancel each other out. To get a better understanding of the differences, we therefore plotted the distribution of our metrics.

As Figure 2 shows, the higher average diversity for the random baseline recommender, but also the user-collaborative recommender, is mainly due to a much flatter distribution with a fatter tail: Even though the peaks of all recommenders are very close to each other,

Table 1. Means and standard deviations distances between topics, tone, category, tags, and from the word 'politiek'.

	Topic	Tone	Category	Tag	Politics
Collab. (item)	90.0 (55.1)	0.14 (0.15)	0.21 (0.23)	0.45 (0.11)	0.79 (0.02)
Semantic (item)	94.4 (56.9)	0.14 (0.14)	0.29 (0.24)	0.46 (0.10)	0.79 (0.02)
Popularity	95.6 (63.8)	0.13 (0.13)	0.00 (0.00)	0.45 (0.10)	0.80 (0.02)
Editors	91.3 (56.6)	0.14 (0.14)	0.10 (0.19)	0.43 (0.10)	0.80 (0.02)
Random	114.6 (68.1)	0.15 (0.15)	0.40 (0.18)	0.52 (0.08)	0.80 (0.02)
Collab. (user)	116.0 (67.0)	0.13 (0.12)	0.37 (0.18)	0.53 (0.07)	0.79 (0.02)
Semantic (user)	96.2 (58.7)	0.14 (0.14)	0.23 (0.24)	0.42 (0.10)	0.79 (0.02)

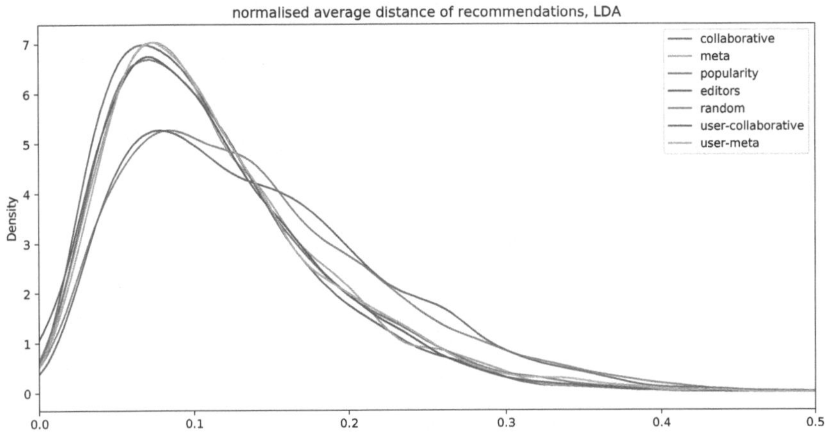

(a)

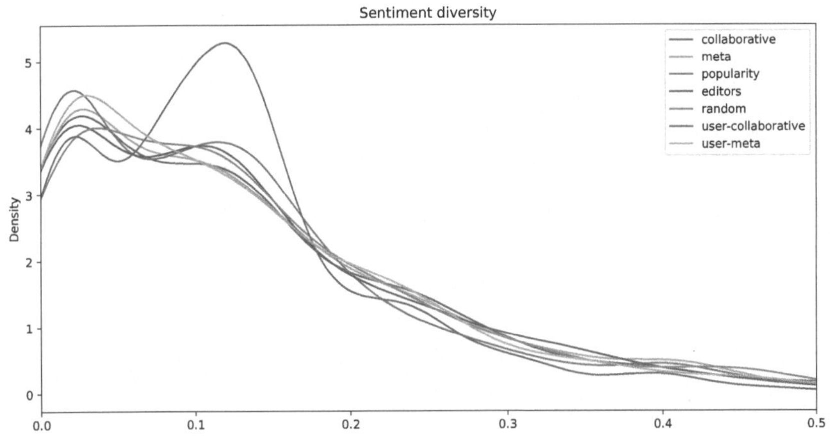

(b)

Figure 2. Topic and sentiment distance. Diversity score distribution of the recommender systems, based on the similarity of (a) LDA topic, and (b) sentiment of a recommended article compared to the currently viewed article.

the random and the user-collaborative recommender more often produce recommendations that are comparatively far off in terms of the LDA topic.

Regarding tone, in line with the descriptive statistics, we do not see many differences, except a hard to explain peak of the user-collaborative recommender.

The distribution of the categories and tags (Figure 3) is quite revealing. As the plot clearly shows human editors are more inclined to simply recommend articles with exactly the same category. Using the other extreme, a random recommender, this hardly happens. Obviously, these random recommendations can be too diverse, indicated by the pronounced tail on the right of the plots. If one aims at providing recommendations from similar, but not always the same categories, it therefore seems to be a good choice to use, for instance, any item-based recommender.

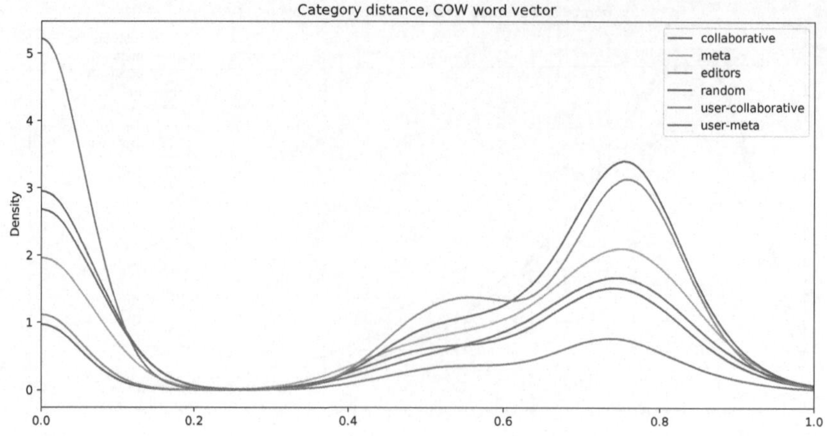

(a)

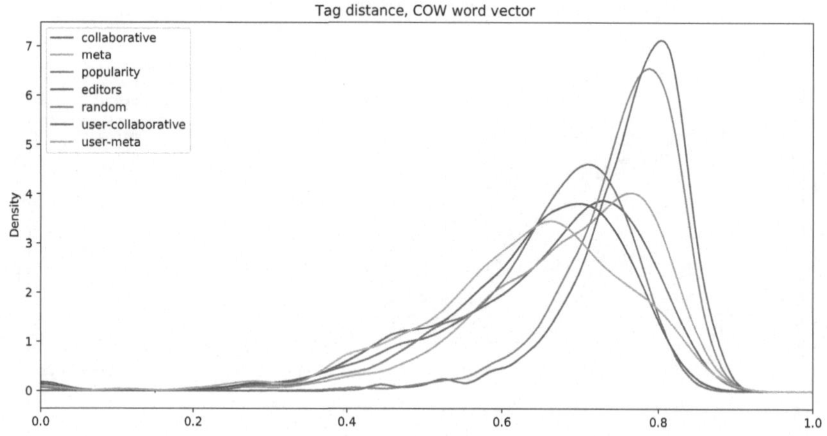

(b)

Figure 3. Category and tag distance. Diversity score distribution of the recommender systems, based on the similarity of (a) category,(b) tags, estimated using word vectors trained on the COW corpus.

Regarding the tags, which are provided by human editors to categorize topics, we see a familiar pattern: The random baseline recommender seems to frequently produce recommendations with very different tags (which is what we would expect), but so does the user-collaborative recommender. The other recommender systems and the editors do not differ much from each other.

Figure 4 indicates that the diversity as in the inclusion of political vs. non-political items does not differ between recommender systems, as we already expected from Table 1. Even though the spikes of the user-collaborative algorithm are more pronounced, they roughly correspond to the peaks of the other algorithms.

Finally, Table 2 and Figure 5 and 6 again illustrate that also if we use formal measures of entropy to assess diversity, we see comparable little differences between the systems – with, as striking exception, the collaborative user-based recommendations that are persistently more diverse than even the random recommendations.

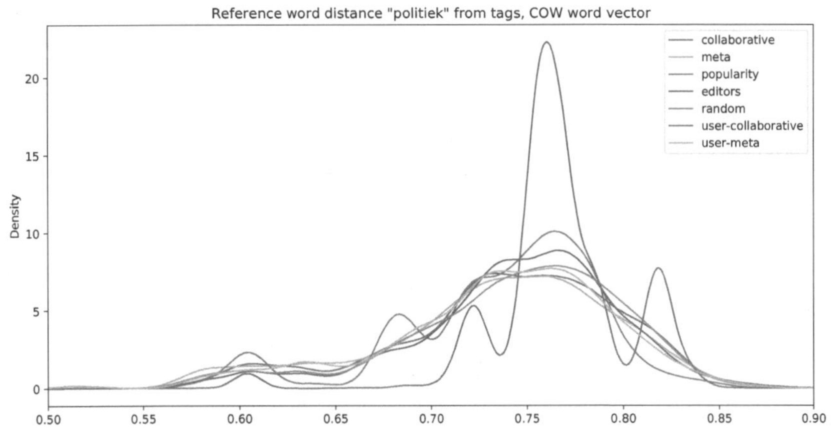

Figure 4. Distance from 'politiek'.

Table 2. Means and standard deviations of diversity metrics using topic distances and category proportions.

	Rao entropy	adapted Rao	Shannon	adapted Shannon
Collaborative (item)	0.0014 (0.0017)	0.08 (0.03)	0.88 (0.28)	0.41 (0.19)
Semantic (item)	0.0012 (0.0013)	0.08 (0.03)	0.85 (0.25)	0.39 (0.17)
Popularity	0.0019 (0.0026)	0.09 (0.03)	0.83 (0.37)	0.38 (0.24)
Editors	0.0014 (0.0019)	0.08 (0.03)	0.81 (0.32)	0.36 (0.20)
Random	0.0012 (0.0013)	0.09 (0.03)	0.83 (0.19)	0.38 (0.24)
Collaborative (user)	0.0018 (0.0016)	0.10 (0.04)	0.95 (0.15)	0.45 (0.10)
Semantic (user)	0.0013 (0.0015)	0.08 (0.03)	0.85 (0.27)	0.38 (0.18)

5. Conclusion and discussion

Our results indicate that news recommendation systems by and large match the diversity of journalistic recommendations. The personalized recommendations showed no reduction in diversity over the non-personalized recommendations; on the contrary, personalized collaborative filtering produced the highest amount of topic diversity in this controlled setting. In sum, we have established that conventional recommendation algorithms at least preserve the topic/sentiment diversity of the article supply.

Having said that, the conventional recommendation algorithms will follow the original distributions, either of the user selections of news, or of the supply of news. We saw that the long-tail was underrepresented. You can imagine that if this was a feedback system based on user selections with a long-tail that is continuously underrepresented, then, naturally, this long-tail will decrease over time. This is statistically unavoidable if no specific measures are taken to protect the long-tail. A truly diversity preserving recommendation engine will rather over-represent the 'minorities' and under-represent the 'majorities' to counter this narrowing effect of the distribution over time. This can be achieved by replacing the proportion in the diversity measures such that niche categories have a larger weight.

The general method that we suggest relies on specific methods for extracting measures like topical distance and tone. These measures can be extended with for instance; complexity, length, writing style, to not only give a diverse recommendation in the sense of meaning

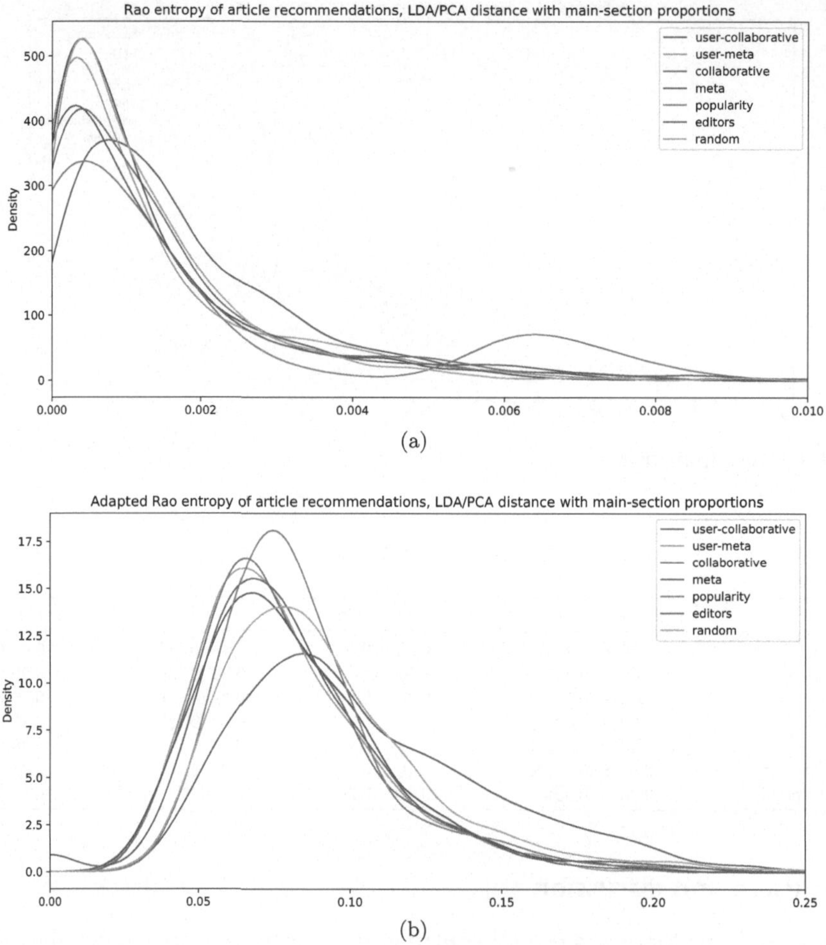

Figure 5. Diversity measure. Distributions for Rao quadratic entropy (a) and adapted Rao quadratic entropy (b).

but also in sense of the effort it takes to read the article. In that sense, we have described a paradigm that, for each measure one chooses to add, one can rely on best-in-class or state-of-the-art methods; it is method-agnostic. We relied on standard LDA for building our topic models. However, very recently, Azarbonyad et al. (2017) have proposed that hierarchical re-estimation of topic models can lead to better estimates of topic diversity. While they are interested in calculating the diversity within a document, we are more interested in differences between documents, future research should evaluate in how far their approach could improve ours. We also demonstrated the use of word embeddings to estimate the similarity of words and even documents. As the quality of these word embeddings relies heavily on the size and relevance of the corpus used to create the embeddings we encourage the generation of public word vectors dedicated to news articles.

The diversity measure we introduced was tested on simulated data from conventional recommendation engines. Next steps are to include our measures in a recommendation engine that is designed to maximize not just for instance the number of articles read or the time spent on them, but also the diversity of the different measures. This

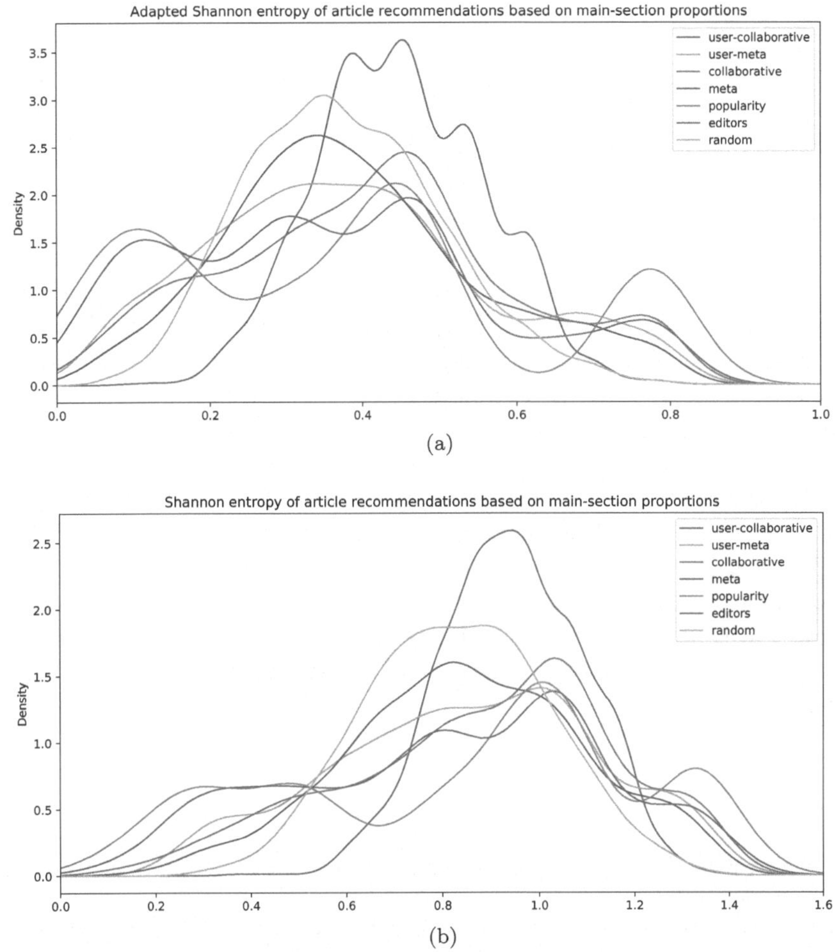

Figure 6. Diversity measure. Distributions for Shannon entropy (a) and adapted Shannon entropy (b).

recommendation engine will assume feedback between the user selections and the user recommendations, and can thus only be tested *in situ*, as such the serendipitous elements of a recommendation system can be used in a smarter way: by providing diverse news that is still relevant to the user.

Future work should explore the different approaches to maximize the diversity and elaborate the different steps that make up our general diversity framework and explore the different options, e.g. for normalizing the feature vectors and combining the features into one feature space that allows for a directional recommendation strategy. It became evident that we need better metrics of diversity to gain a better understanding of the true impact of recommender systems. To better understand the impact of these recommendation engines and whether over time there is indeed a reduction of content diversity these difference recommendation engines should be tested *in situ* over a longer period of several months. The current work should be seen in the context of the development of diversity metrics for the evaluation of recommendation engines.

It is important to note that our analyses are based on a pool of articles that were published in a high-quality broadsheet paper in one country. That means the pool of articles was quite diverse in terms of topic and tone, but only to a small extent in categories that we did not analyze (e.g. style or viewpoints). To get a better understanding of the influence of recommender systems on society at large, we need to replicate this study for a larger and more diverse pool of news. Similarly, our finding that recommender systems preserve diversity needs to be explored further. It could be that the negative effects of filter bubbles are caused not by recommenders that recommend self-enforcing information, but by repetitively showing a set of information snippets of which the most cognitive-consonant is most likely selected, which in time will lead to a narrowing of the recommended set. That means, future work on news recommendation systems needs to incorporate the notion of personalization over time, especially with regard to long-term effects of recommendations on the overall structure of information markets.

As such, this paper should be understood as a stepping stone into researching diversity as an outcome of recommendation systems as the rich and relevant concept it really is. As more and more users are receiving their news through these recommendation systems, be it on a social medium, news compilers integrated in automatic personal assistants, or on legacy news media homepages, it is crucial to understand and monitor how diverse the news menus are that are offered to the user, acknowledging that diverse can mean a lot of different things.

Notes

1. A different approach could be to compare the recommendations for different people (see also Haim et al., 2017).
2. First, we calculate the Euclidean distance for all topic pairs, resulting in a fully symmetric 50×50 matrix **M**, which we call our topic dissimilarity matrix. Second, we multiply **M** with $\vec{w_{D1}}$ and $\vec{w_{D2}}$, for document 1 and 2 respectively, resulting in two matrices **A** and **B**,

$$\mathbf{A} = \mathrm{M}\sqrt{\vec{w_{D1}}\vec{w_{D1}}^{\mathrm{T}}}, \quad \mathbf{B} = \mathrm{M}\sqrt{\vec{\mathbf{w_{D2}}}\vec{\mathbf{w_{D2}}}^{\mathrm{T}}} \tag{3}$$

which represent the topic dissimilarity matrices weighed by the topic occurrence in the document in question. These matrices **A** and **B** contain mixed terms such as $M_{21}w_1$ which are ambiguous since it does not include the weight for one of the topics in the pair. To discard these mixed terms, we need to rewrite the above formulation to

$$\mathbf{A} = \mathrm{diag}(\mathrm{M})\mathcal{I}\sqrt{\vec{\mathbf{w_{D1}}}\vec{\mathbf{w_{D1}}}^{\mathrm{T}}} + (\mathrm{M} - \mathrm{diag}(\mathrm{M})\mathcal{I})\sqrt{\vec{\mathrm{w_{D1}}}\vec{\mathrm{w_{D1}}}^{\mathrm{T}}} - \mathrm{diag}\left(\sqrt{\vec{\mathrm{w_{D1}}}\vec{\mathrm{w_{D1}}}^{\mathrm{T}}}\right)\mathcal{I} \tag{4}$$

We can then calculate the Euclidian distance. We assume that each feature space has the same bounds, hence all feature spaces need to be normalized before being combined between the two matrices using the Frobenius norm: topical distance between two documents $= \|A - B\|_{\mathrm{F}} = \sqrt{\sum_{i=1}^{m}\sum_{j=1}^{n}|a_{ij} - b_{ij}|^2}$.

Disclosure statement

No potential conflict of interest was reported by the authors.

Funding

This work was supported by the European Research Council, ERC-grant 638514, and the Research Priority Area of the University of Amsterdam. It was carried out on the Dutch national e-infrastructure with the support of SURF Foundation.

Notes on contributors

Judith Möller is a postdoctoral researcher at the Amsterdam School of Communication Research. In her research she focuses on the effects of political communication, in particular social media and digital media [email: J.E.Moller1@uva.nl].

Damian Trilling is an Assistant Professor at the Department of Communication Science and affiliated with the Amsterdam School of Communication Research. He is intrigued by the question how citizens nowadays are informed about current affairs and events in their society [email: d.c.trilling@uva.nl].

Natali Helberger is professor in Information Law at the Institute for Information Law. She specializes in the regulation of converging information and communications markets. Focus points of her research are the interface between technology and information law, user rights and the changing role of the user in information law and policy [email: n.helberger@uva.nl].

Bram van Es works is a Research Engineer at the eScience Centre, Amsterdam. He holds a PhD in Physics and has extensive experience in data analysis and machine learning. He has co-developed the a plugin to collect tracking data, the data pipeline and the analysis library for the personalised communication project [email: bramiozo@gmail.com].

References

Azarbonyad, H., Dehghani, M., Kenter, T., Marx, M., Kamps, J., & De Rijke, M. (2017). Hierarchical re-estimation of topic models for measuring topical diversity. In J. M. Jose, C. Hauff, I. S. Altıngovde, D. Song, D. Albakour, S. Watt, & J. Tait (Eds.), *Advances in information retrieval: 39th European Conference on IR research (ECIR 2017), Aberdeen, UK* (pp. 68–81). Cham: Springer.

Bakshy, E., Messing, S., & Adamic, L. A. (2015). Exposure to ideologically diverse news and opinion on Facebook. *Science*, *348*(6239), 1130–1132.

Beam, M. A. (2014). Automating the news: How personalized news recommender system design choices impact news reception. *Communication Research*, *41*(8), 1019–1041.

Benson, R. (2009). What makes news more multiperspectival? A field analysis. *Poetics*, *37*(5), 402–418.

Blei, D., Ng, A., & Jordan, M. (2003). Latent Dirichlet allocation. *Journal of Machine Learning Research*, *3*, 993–1022.

Bozdag, E. (2013). Bias in algorithmic filtering and personalization. *Ethics and Information Technology*, *15*(3), 209–227.

Bridge, D., & Kelly, J. P. (2006). Ways of computing diverse collaborative recommendations. In International conference on adaptive hypermedia and adaptive web-based systems (pp. 41–50). Springer.

De Smedt, T., & Daelemans, W. (2012). Pattern for Python. *The Journal of Machine Learning Research*, *13*, 2063–2067.

Duncan, J., & Reid, J. (2013). Toward a measurement tool for the monitoring of media diversity and pluralism in South Africa: A public-centred approach. *Communication*, *39*(4), 483–500.

Dylko, I. B. (2016). How technology encourages political selective exposure. *Communication Theory*, *26*(4), 389–409.

Dylko, I. B., Dolgov, I., Hoffman, W., Eckhart, N., Molina, M., & Aaziz, O. (2017). The dark side of technology: An experimental investigation of the influence of customizability technology on online political selective exposure. *Computers in Human Behavior*, *73*, 181–190.

Ferree, M. M., Gamson, W. A., Gerhards, J., & Rucht, D. (2002). Four models of the public sphere in modern democracies. *Theory and Society*, *31*(3), 289–324.

Flaxman, S. R., & Rao, J. M. (2016). Filter bubbles, echo chambers, and online news consumption. *Public Opinion Quarterly*, *80*, 298–320.

Fletcher, R., & Nielsen, R. K. (2017). Are news audiences increasingly fragmented? A cross-national comparative analysis of cross-platform news audience fragmentation and duplication. *Journal of Communication*, *67*(4), 476–498.

Haim, M., Graefe, A., & Brosius, H.-B. (2017). Burst of the filter bubble? Effects of personalization on the diversity of Google News. *Digital Journalism*, 1–14.

Helberger, N., Karppinen, K., & D'Acunto, L. (2018). Exposure diversity as a design principle for recommender systems. *Information, Communication & Society*, *21*(2), 191–207.

Junqué de Fortuny, E., De Smedt, T., Martens, D., & Daelemans, W. (2012). Media coverage in times of political crisis: A text mining approach. *Expert Systems with Applications*, *39*(14), 11616–11622.

Karppinen, K. (2013). *Rethinking media pluralism. Donald McGannon Research Center*. New York, NY: Fordham University Press.

Karppinen, K. (2015). The limits of empirical indicators: Media pluralism as an essentially contested concept. In P. Valcke, M. Sükösd, & R. G. Picard (Eds.), *Media pluralism and diversity* (pp. 287–296). London: Palgrave Macmillan.

Kitchin, R. (2017). Thinking critically about and researching algorithms. *Information, Communication & Society*, *20*(1), 14–29.

Knijnenburg, B. P., Willemsen, M. C., Gantner, Z., Soncu, H., & Newell, C. (2012). Explaining the user experience of recommender systems. *User Modeling and User-Adapted Interaction*, *22*(4–5), 441–504.

Kotkov, D., Wang, S., & Veijalainen, J. (2016). A survey of serendipity in recommender systems. *Knowledge-Based Systems*, *111*(Supplement C), 180–192.

Kunaver, M., & Požrl, T. (2017). Diversity in recommender systems – a survey. *Knowledge-Based Systems*, *123*(Supplement C), 154–162.

Masini, A., Aelst, P. V., Zerback, T., Reinemann, C., Mancini, P., Mazzoni, M., Damiani, M., & Coen, S. (2017). Measuring and explaining the diversity of voices and viewpoints in the news. *Journalism Studies*, *54*, 1–20.

Napoli, P. M. (2015). Assessing media diversity in the US: A comparative analysis of the FCC's diversity index and the EU's media pluralism monitor. In P. Valcke, M. Sükösd, & R. G. Picard (Eds.), *Media pluralism and diversity*. London: Palgrave. Assessing media diversity in the US: A comparative analysis of the FCC's diversity index and the EU's media pluralism monitor. In Media pluralism and diversity (pp. 141–151). Springer.

O'Callaghan, D., Greene, D., Conway, M., Carthy, J., & Cunningham, P. (Aug 2015). Down the (white) rabbit hole: The extreme right and online recommender systems. *Social Science Computer Review*, *33*(4), 459–478.

Owen, D., & Smith, G. (2015). Survey article: Deliberation, democracy, and the systemic turn. *Journal of Political Philosophy*, *23*(2), 213–234.

Pariser, E. (2011). *The filter bubble: What the internet is hiding from you*. New York, NY: Penguin.

Council of Europe (2007). Recommendation Rec(2007)2 of the committee of ministers to member states on media pluralism and diversity of media content.

Řehůřek, R., & Sojka, P. (2010). Software framework for topic modelling with large corpora. In *Proceedings of the LREC 2010 workshop on new challenges for NLP frameworks* (pp. 45–50). ELRA, Valletta, Malta. Retrieved from http://is.muni.cz/publication/884893/en.

Ribeiro, M. T., Ziviani, N., Moura, E. S. D., Hata, I., Lacerda, A., & Veloso, A. (2015). Multiobjective pareto-efficient approaches for recommender systems. *ACM Transactions on Intelligent Systems and Technology (TIST)*, *5*(4), 53.

Ricci, F., Rokach, L., & Shapira, B. (2011). Introduction to recommender systems handbook. In F. Ricci, L. Rokach, & B. Shapira (Eds.), *Recommender systems handbook* (pp. 1–35). New York, NY: Springer.

Ricotta, C., & Szeidl, L. (2006). Towards a unifying approach to diversity measures: Bridging the gap between the Shannon entropy and Rao's quadratic index. *Theoretical Population Biology, 70*(3), 237–243.

Schäfer, R., & Bildhauer, F. (2012). Building large corpora from the web using a new efficient tool chain. In Proceedings of the tenth international conference on language resources and evaluation (LREC 2012) (pp. 486–493), Istanbul, Turkey.

Shoemaker, P. J., Eichholz, M., Kim, E., & Wrigley, B. (2001). Individual and routine forces in gatekeeping. *Journalism & Mass Communication Quarterly, 78*(2), 233–246.

Sievert, C., & Shirley, K. (2014). LDAvis: A method for visualizing and interpreting topics. In *Proceedings of the workshop on interactive language learning, visualization, and interfaces* (pp. 63–70). Retrieved from http://www.aclweb.org/anthology/W/W14/W14-3110.

Smyth, B., & McClave, P. (2001). Similarity vs. diversity. In International conference on case-based reasoning (pp. 347–361). Springer, Vancouver, Canada.

Sørensen, J. K., & Schmidt, J. -H. (2016). *An algorithmic diversity diet? Questioning assumptions behind a diversity recommendation system for PSM.* Working paper, Hans-Bredow-Institute for Media Research, Hamburg, Germany.

Strömbäck, J. (2005). In search of a standard: Four models of democracy and their normative implications for journalism. *Journalism Studies, 6*(3), 331–345.

Stroud, N. J. (2011). *Niche news: The politics of news choice.* New York, NY: Oxford University Press.

Sunstein, C. R. (2007). *Republic.com 2.0.* Princeton, NJ: Princeton University Press.

Tulkens, S., Emmery, C., & Daelemans, W. (2016). Evaluating unsupervised Dutch word embeddings as a linguistic resource. In N. Calzolari, K. Choukri, T. Declerck, M. Grobelnik, B. Maegaard, J. Mariani, A. Moreno, J. Odijk, & S. Piperidis (Eds.), *Proceedings of the tenth international conference on language resources and evaluation (LREC 2016). European Language Resources Association (ELRA)*, Paris, France.

Van Cuilenburg, J. (1999). On competition, access and diversity in media, old and new: Some remarks for communications policy in the information age. *New Media & Society, 1*(2), 183–207.

Willemsen, M. C., Graus, M. P., & Knijnenburg, B. P. (2016). Understanding the role of latent feature diversification on choice difficulty and satisfaction. *User Modeling and User-Adapted Interaction, 26*(4), 347–389.

Ziegler, C.-N., McNee, S. M., Konstan, J. A., & Lausen, G. (2005). Improving recommendation lists through topic diversification. In Proceedings of the 14th international conference on World Wide Web (WWW '05). ACM Press, (PP. 22–32), Chiba, Japan.

Zuiderveen Borgesius, F. J., Trilling, D., Möller, J., Bodó, B., De Vreese, C. H., & Helberger, N. (2016). Should we worry about filter bubbles? *Internet Policy Review, 5*(1).

4 Women politicians are more engaging

Male versus female politicians' ability to generate users' engagement on social media during an election campaign

Moran Yarchi and Tal Samuel-Azran

ABSTRACT

In light of past studies' findings that male politicians usually receive more salient coverage in the traditional media, this study examines whether social media provide a more equal opportunity platform for female politicians to generate users' engagement and mobilize their supporters. Our study focuses on male versus female politicians' ability to engage social media users during an election campaign, using the Israeli 2015 campaign as our case study. Female politicians' posts generated significantly more user engagement in terms of the number of Likes and Shares in comparison to male politicians, while generating the same number of participants in their discussions. The results remained significant in a multilevel analysis, while controlling for other factors such as the politician's age, party, ranking, and number of posts published by the politician. In terms of the posts' content, an examination of their rhetoric did not reveal gender differences in their usage of authoritative voice, facts, and the use of emotions in their messages; however, analysis of the topics did suggest differences in the issues raised by male versus female politicians. The evidence strongly indicates that social media provides greater opportunities for female politicians to promote themselves and improve their status in the political power play.

Introduction

The question of whether women have fair opportunity, compared to men, to enter political life is a central issue in contemporary political studies (e.g., Basow, 2016; Joiner et al., 2016). While the majority of studies dealing with female politicians' ability to attract media attention have focused on traditional media (e.g., Bystrom, Robertson, & Banwart, 2001; Everitt, Best, & Gaudet, 2016), their ability to promote themselves via social media - currently a central stage for political discourse - has been somewhat neglected. While in the last decade, increasing scholarly attention has been paid to candidates' use of social media (Bronstein, 2013; Metzgar & Maruggi, 2009; Samuel-Azran, Yarchi, & Wolfsfeld, 2015; Wolfsfeld, Yarchi, & Samuel-Azran, 2016), few have addressed the gender factor. The current study aims to address this lacuna by examining female politicians' ability to generate users' engagement and mobilize their supporters through social media, in comparison to the ability of male politicians, during an election campaign.

Accordingly, the current study aims to expand the understanding regarding politicians' use of social media, while focusing on gender differences; specifically, we aim to examine the ability of male and female politicians to generate users' engagement in their social media posts during an election campaign. Using the Israeli 2015 parliamentary election campaign as our case study, we analyze differences in the extent to which male versus female politicians were able to engage Facebook members (in terms of number of Likes, Shares, comments, and participation in discussions). In addition, the rhetoric used by the politicians in their posts is examined. Specifically, we examine the extent to which male and female politicians were able to promote engagement with messages posted on their official Facebook pages during one of the most critical points of their election campaigns: the week leading to Election Day. We chose to focus on politicians' Facebook posts during the 2015 Israeli election campaign since Facebook is the most popular social network in Israel (Alexa, 2016) and is frequently used by politicians to convey messages to the public (Kabir & Urbach, 2013).[1] Already in 2010, an examination of Israeli politicians' online activity revealed that most (70%, or 84 out of 120) Israeli parliamentary members maintained a presence on Facebook (Haleva-Amir, 2011; Livak, Lev-On, & Doron, 2011); since then, the number of active politicians on social media has grown even further (Lev-On & Haleva-Amir, 2018).

The topic of the study is particularly relevant because traditional media usually tend to perpetuate the perception that politics is a more masculine field of interest and profession, while male politicians usually receive more salient coverage compared to female politicians (e.g., Basow, 2016; Braden, 1996; Bystrom et al., 2001; Everitt et al., 2016). In contrast, recent studies have indicated that social media could provide a more equal platform for female politicians, as studies have found that social media provide a more supportive environment for women compared to men as women are much more likely than men to respond to public messages and to Like contents (Joiner et al., 2016) as well as support each other (Wang, Burke, & Kraut, 2013), aspects that could potentially facilitate female politicians in promoting engagement and support for their messages. In the current study, we aim to examine whether social media does indeed provide a more equal ground with regard to gender differences in politics. In other words, we ask: Do female politicians generate the same amount of users' engagement on social media as their male peers?

Gender bias and stereotypes in the media

Whereas historically women around the world were not allowed to vote or run for parliament (Andersen, 1996), the participation of women politicians in governments globally increased steadily during the twentieth century. Indeed, in some regions, such as northern Europe (specifically Finland, Iceland, Sweden, and Switzerland), and countries such as Rwanda and Bolivia, female politicians comprise between a third to half or more of the parliament (UN Women, 2017). In the US, the increased number of women running for office was assigned to organizations like 'She Should Run' and 'VoteRunLead' which encourage women to run for government offices. However, from a wider perspective, the percentage of female politicians' participation in parliaments globally is still low, standing at only 22.8% (UN Women, 2017).

In Israel, there are only 4 females out of 23 ministers, and only 33 females out of the 120 Knesset members (27.5%), in the (current) Twentieth Knesset (whose members were elected on 17 March 2015 and sworn in on 31 March 2015). It is an improvement in comparison to the 9 female Knesset members the country had about 20 years ago – but it portrays that Israel represents a country that is still far from equal representation of women in politics and is far behind countries like Norway, Sweden, or Iceland with over 40% representation of women in parliament. The situation is also grim in the leaders' roles department: although Golda Meir served as the Prime Minister of Israel before the 1969 elections following the death of Levi Eshkol, and ended her job in 1974, it took another 12 years until another woman was appointed as a minister with a portfolio, and 18 years until a woman was appointed to any other portfolio, Education Minister.

Beyond this relatively low numerical representation, recent studies have found that elected female politicians and candidates are still subject to processes of gender stereotyping (Basow, 2016; Brescoll, 2016; Everitt et al., 2016), noting that female politicians face stereotypical questions on womanhood in the media in a manner that is similar to the gender stereotyping a few decades ago (Braden, 1996; Gidengil & Everitt, 1999). The persistent stereotyping of female politicians has been primarily expressed in two main realms: volume of representation and type of representation. In terms of volume, already in 1996, Kahn's content analysis found that women running for office in the United States systematically received less media coverage compared to men. Braden's (1996) and Bystrom et al.'s (2001) analyses of the media coverage of female and male candidates in primary races for governor and US Senate in 2000 identified a similar gender bias trend. Global studies in central countries have further reinforced the notion that, in most cases, the volume bias against female politicians persists. For example, Ross, Evans, Harrison, Shears, and Wadia's (2013) analysis of politicians' representation during the 2010 British elections revealed that female politicians are much less likely to feature in news stories compared to male politicians, while Hooghe, Jacobs, and Claes (2015) showed that female politicians are significantly less likely to be allotted speaking time compared to their male colleagues. In terms of the type of the representation, studies have shown that when female politicians are mentioned, the articles often focus explicitly on gender issues, thus posing them as interesting based on their sex, rather than their political abilities (Ross et al., 2013). Thus, the representation of female politicians has focused more on physical appearance and personal life (Bystrom et al., 2001; Ross et al., 2013) and less on issues and political ideas, thereby reducing the ability of females to present themselves as viable candidates (Aday & Devitt, 2001). Indeed, a large study on Israeli media's reporting of women involvement in local politics in Israel between 1950 and 1989 identified that the reporting was shaped by the exclusionary social frames that rest on the dichotomous notion of masculine/public/political versus feminine/private/apolitical representation (Herzog, 1998).

Importantly, recent studies argue that the gendered stereotyping has decreased, as indicated in a series of studies by Hayes and Lawless (2015) and Hayes, Lawless, and Baltinger (2014) which bring counter-evidence to the gender stereotyping argument. Wasburn and Wasburn (2011) found that Sarah Palin even gained a higher volume of representation compared to her male counterparts in the 2008 US presidential elections.

Social media and female politicians

In contrast to the biased representation in traditional media, which potentially harms female politicians, several studies have indicated that social media allows women to support each other, and thus might serve as a supportive environment for female politicians. In a recent study, Joiner et al. (2016) indicated that females tend to support other females publicly on social media significantly more often than males support males. These findings match Wang et al.'s (2013) study that identified topics from more than half a million Facebook status updates, revealing that women generally receive more feedback compared to men. These findings are compatible with studies that have examined motives for social network site use, and found that females are more likely to report high positive collective self-esteem and greater overall use and use the networks to communicate with peers (Patti, Valkenburg, & Schouten, 2006). In Israel, the subject of the current study, Hayat, Lesser, and Samuel-Azran's (2017) study found that women more often commented on other peoples' posts, females' posts received higher ranking than those of males, and females belonged to more active networks. These findings are also supported by a poll conducted by the advertising firm McCann Ericson in 2016, which revealed that nearly 80% of Israeli women are members of social networks online and they are more active and supportive of each other compared to men, as 73% of women in the poll said they followed their friends' posts regularly, versus only 53% of men (Peer, 2016).

However, at the same time, it is important to note that some evidence contradicts the notion that female politicians benefit from online social network environments more than males. Brandtzaeg (2015) found that males are more drawn toward political and information-oriented subjects compared to females, who are more strongly attracted to private issues and thus might be less interested in engaging with female politicians' posts and leave political discussions on social networks mostly to men. In addition, studies have identified that males' tendency to dominate conversations (Lakoff, 1975) spills into the online realm as well (Armento-Cota, 2011). Hayat et al.'s (2017) analysis identified that Israeli male start more threads and write more posts than their female counterparts, concluding that this could indicate males' dominance of conversations and leadership roles in online social network discussions.

The above-mentioned studies have not specifically addressed female versus male politicians' ability to engage social network users during elections, which is the subject of our study. We found very few studies dealing with female politicians in social media. The most notable is McGregor and Mourão's (2016) network analysis of Twitter conversations during the 2014 United States House of Representatives elections, which found that when a woman opposes a man, the Twitter conversation usually revolves around her rather than her male counterpart, indicating that the power of female politicians' connections within the networks examined is stronger than that of their male counterparts. Interestingly, the study found that this effect disappeared when women opposed women. Additional evidence for the ability of social media to empower female candidates comes from Erikson's (2008) study, which identified that social networking sites allowed Hillary Clinton to maintain close interaction with supporters, many of them females, who advised her regarding her campaign slogans throughout her 2008 election campaign.

In contrast, a study that examined party leaders' ability to engage social media users during the 2013 elections in Israel (Samuel-Azran, Yarchi, & Wolfsfeld, 2016) found that overall Israeli male party leaders' Facebook posts gained dramatically more engagement than those of their female counterparts. In addition, McGregor and Mourão (2016) noted that despite their findings (noted above) regarding female politicians' centrality on Twitter, gender bias sometimes still exists on the platform, as illustrated in the 'Abortion Barbie' hashtag that Twitter followers created for Texas Democratic candidate Wendy Davis, an outspoken critic of abortion, based on her fashionable and stylish appearance.

The gender bias problem expressed in the above realms is even further extended when we look at the literature on gender and language, particularly in the context of leadership (e.g., Cameron, 2006; Koller, 2004; Mills, 2006; Wodak, 1997), which has shown that leadership is conceptualized as intrinsically masculine. The prevailing stereotype assumes that an 'effective' leader is one whose behavior and language is authoritative, assertive, adversarial, competitive, task-focused, goal-orientated, and single-minded (Bass, 1998; Sinclair, 1998), thus singling out women who do not conform to these standards as not fit to be leaders (Priola & Brannen, 2009; Schnurr, 2009). The notion that females, including those in leadership roles, are inherently different in their language use than their male counterparts fits within the 'different voice' (Gilligan, 1982) paradigm, which suggests that females and males use a different language.

However, the 'different voice' paradigm has been widely challenged in the last two decades. According to Baxter (2011), who studied the language of UK women business leaders, the structured disadvantage of the soft and submissive voice leads female leaders to adopt a 'double-voiced' discourse, wherein they adjust what they say to fit the male-dominated institutional environment in order to thrive in their institution's atmosphere. Baxter's arguments fit within the wider findings that in various male-dominated institutions, from the police (McElhinny, 1995) to the Anglican Church (Walsh, 2001) to the British House of Commons (Shaw, 2000), females imitate the institution's speech styles, which are highly affected by the male-dominated language to fit within the institution's culture. Furthermore, and interestingly, the 'double-voice' notion argument has been strengthened in the last two decades as many male leaders - most notably Bill Clinton, Tony Blair, and Barack Obama - have started to combine their traditional authoritative masculine voice with feminine aspects of expressing emotions and empathy in a manner that makes them appear more sincere and authentic, in line with the blurring gender roles in our time (Cameron & Shaw, 2016). Indeed, Cameron and Shaw's (2016) study of female language styles in the 2015 general elections in the United Kingdom showed that female politicians combined authoritative voice with emotional voice. Analysis of Hillary Clinton's rhetoric during the 2016 US elections campaign also indicated a combination of authoritative voice; for example, in combining aggressive attacks on Trump with a softer, more feminine voice emphasizing the theme of motherhood (Kenty, 2016). Thus, in recent years, the rhetoric used and the topics discussed by male and female politicians have tended to be similar.

While the above studies have pointed out the interplay of gender and language in various realms, only a few studies have dealt with the issue of female politicians and social media, and none of these have compared male and female politicians' ability to promote themselves by engaging their followers. The current study aims to address this gap, using the Israeli 2015 parliamentary elections campaign as a case study.

To sum, literature in the field has suggested that politics is considered a masculine field of interest, and that while dealing with the media's coverage of politicians, men tend to receive more attention compared to women (Basow, 2016; Braden, 1996; Bystrom et al., 2001; Everitt et al., 2016). On the other hand, while dealing with social media, newer studies have indicated that it serves as a more comfortable and supportive environment for women (Joiner et al., 2016; Wang et al., 2013). Thus, our research question (RQ1) asks: *Does social media set an equal ground for female politicians to engage (in terms of the number of Likes, Shares, comments, and participants in discussions) with the public, in comparison to their male peers?*

In terms of message content, recent studies have found that in today's reality, both male and female politicians tend to speak in a similar voice, without emphasizing gender differences in their rhetoric or topics discussed. Politicians' messages today express 'double-voiced' discourse, presenting the stereotypically male authoritative voice alongside the stereotypically female emotional language (Cameron & Shaw, 2016; Kenty, 2016). Thus, we can expect that both male and female politicians will use a similar rhetoric in their election campaigns through social media - combining authoritative voice (ethos) with emotional language (pathos) - and deal with similar topics in their posts. The study's hypothesis (H1) is that *Male and female politicians' social media posts during an election campaign will present similar topics and rhetoric in terms of authoritative and emotional messages.*

Method

To examine the differences in the level of engagement male and female politicians generate on social media, we measured users' participation and engagement in politicians' posts on Facebook during eight days of the 2015 Israeli elections campaign - the week leading to the elections themselves and elections day. As mentioned above, we focus on Facebook - the most popular social network in Israel (Alexa, 2016) - which is heavily used by Israeli politicians in an attempt to convey their messages and engage with their supporters (Haleva-Amir, 2011; Kabir & Urbach, 2013; Livak et al., 2011).

In order to obtain a better understanding of the Israeli political environment, it is important to define its political system. Israel has a multiparty proportionate representation system, which has always led to the formation of coalition governments (in the current Parliament, the Twentieth Knesset, there are representatives of 10 parties, 6 of which formed the ruling government). Israeli citizens vote for their preferred party; however, due to the tendency in Western democratic countries to emphasize and personalize candidates (Balmas, Rahat, Sheafer, & Shenhav, 2014), and changes made to the Israeli voting system,[2] candidates play a significant role in election campaigns.

This study examines the Twentieth Israeli Parliament (the Knesset) elections, held on 17 March 2015. We analyzed all messages posted on 33 politicians' (14 women and 19 men) official Facebook pages between 10 March 2015 (a week before Election Day) and 17 March 2015 (Election Day). Altogether, eight days were analyzed (the week leading to Election Day and Election Day itself). We examined the amount of engagement the politicians had generated in terms of the number of Likes and Shares each post had received, as well as the number of comments to each post and the number of participants in each discussion (users that had commented on the posts). In line with the structure of

Israel's multiparty system, our analysis included all female politicians ranked within the first 10 places of their party for the two major political parties (the Likud and the Zionist Camp - a party uniting the Labor and The Movement parties), and all female politicians ranked in the first five places of their party for the remainder of the parties. For each female politician examined, we sampled a matching male politician from the same party and in the same political position (the male politician ranked right before or after the female politician on the same party's list - for example, a female politician ranked fourth and a male politician ranked fifth in the Zionist Camp party's list),[3] in order to control for the level of popularity among their supporters and the newsworthiness of the politicians. In addition, we had added six male party leaders to our sample – thus, all party leaders that their party had passed the threshold and were elected for the Knesset, besides Prime Minister Netanyahu, appeared in our analysis. Our decision not to include Prime Minister Netanyahu in our sample is based on previous studies findings, which claim (according to the normalization hypothesis) that during an election campaign, the incumbent has an advantage and generate more engagement on social media (Koc-Michalska, Gibson, & Vedel, 2014; Lev-On & Haleva-Amir, 2018)[4] – thus, it would not be an appropriate comparison to the engagement generated by other politicians, regardless of their

Table 1. The politicians examined and the number of posts they had published.

Female politician	Ranking in their party's list	No. of posts	Male politician	Ranking in their party's list	No. of posts	Party
Miri Regev	5th	28	Israel Katz	4th	7	The Likud
Tzipi Livni	2nd	18	Yitzhak Herzog	1st	32	The Zionist Camp
Shelly Yachimovich	3rd	18	–			The Zionist Camp
Stav Shaffir	4th	10	Itzik Shmuli	5th	11	The Zionist Camp
Merav Michaeli	9th	14	Amir Preretz,	8th	16	The Zionist Camp
Aida Touma-Sliman	5th	6	Abd Al Hakeem Haj Yahya	6th	0	The Joint List
Yael German	5th	8	Shay Piron	4th	4	Yesh Atid
Rachel Azaria	5th	0	Michael Oren	4th	5	Kulanu
Ayelet Shaked	4th	31	Uri Ariel	3rd	13	The Jewish Home
Orly Levi-Abekasis	2nd	16	Avigdor Lieberman	1st	21	Yisrael Beytenu
Sofa Landver	3rd	11	Sharon Gal	4th	13	Yisrael Beytenu
Zehava Galon	1st	20	Ilan Gilon	2nd	11	Meretz
Michal Rozin	4th	8	Esawi Frej	3rd	4	Meretz
Tamar Zandberg	5th	8	Mossi Raz	6th	18	Meretz
Additional party leaders						
			Yair Lapid	1st	35	Yesh Atid
			Naftali Bennett	1st	69	The Jewish Home
			Moshe kahlon	1st	29	Kulanu
			Ayman Odeh	1st	6	The Joint List
			Arie Drei	1st	11	Shas
			Yaakov Litzman	1st	0	Yahadut Hatorah

Note: Two ultra-orthodox parties Shas and Yahadut Hatorah did not have any female politicians on their lists, and were represented only by their party leaders in the current study.

gender. The politicians examined, their party affiliation and ranking, and the number of posts they had published during the week leading to Election Day are presented in Table 1.

All data were collected using Buzzilla's software, an Israeli social media and online representation trend-tracking company. The politicians' posts as appeared on their official Facebook pages ($N = 501$[5]) were examined. Out of the 33 politicians examined in the study, 30 had communicated with their audience using their Facebook page during the week leading to the elections (three politicians, Yaakov Litzman, Rachel Azaria, and Abd Al Hakeem Haj Yahya, did not post any messages on their Facebook page during the time of our examination[6]). In addition to the politician official Facebook pages, we had retrieved information about their online traditional media appearances, in order to examine the salience of male versus female politicians in the Israeli media. Altogether 11,648 articles dealing with the politicians we had used in our analysis were published during the week leading to the elections and on Election Day (the time frame of our analysis): 9263 of those articles had dealt with the 19 male politicians examined in the study, while only 2385 had dealt with the 14 female politicians sampled.

In order to get a broader understanding of the ways in which male and female politicians generate users' engagement with their communications via Facebook, we examined other factors that serve as control variables in the current study. These include (a) the politician's party, understanding that different parties tend to generate different amount of user engagement (Yarchi, Wolfsfeld, Samuel-Azran, & Segev, 2017); (b) the politician's age, assuming that younger politicians, like younger people, are more social media-oriented (Vromen, Xenos, & Loader, 2015); (c) the politician's ranking in the party's list, since politicians' political status may affect their popularity[7] (Lev-On & Haleva-Amir, 2018); (d) the number of posts published by the politician during the week leading to Election Day; and (e) how many days before the elections the post was published. As for our dependent variable, three indicators were used in order to examine user engagement with the politicians' posts: (a) the number of Likes a post received; (b) the number of Shares a post received (the number of people willing to repost that message on their Facebook wall); and (c) the comments that each post had generated – examining both the number of comments and the number of participants in the discussions following each post (Rather than looking only at the number of comments, which can be misleading as a measurement of engagement since the same user can comment more than once on each post, we had also looked at the number of unique users/participants who wrote the comments). Combined, these three indicators provide a broad overview of users' engagement on Facebook. The number of participants indicates how many people engaged in a discussion about the politician, while both the Likes and Shares serve as indicators of popularity. The Share indicator contributes to an understanding of the discussion surrounding a given message, as a share represents greater user commitment than other engagement indicators (Malhotra, Malhotra, & See, 2013) and willingness to post the message on their Facebook page. Since the variables were examined on two different levels (post and politician), we used a multilevel analysis in order to get a more accurate assessment of politicians' ability to generate users' engagement on social media.

In addition, to provide another dimension to the study and better understand the differences in politicians' output, rather than just the reception of the messages, the content of 27 politicians' posts was examined using content analysis (the paired politicians for the same party and at a similar ranking). The rhetoric used by the politicians in their messages, and the topics they dealt with, were examined with the aim of obtaining a better understanding of the messages politicians published on their social media ($N = 301^{8}$). The Aristotelian discourse analysis method builds on Aristotle's classic essay 'Rhetoric', widely considered the most important single work on persuasion ever written. The essay offers speakers three powerful and distinctly different persuasive appeals: ethos, logos, and pathos (Golden, Berquist, Coleman, Golden, & Sproule, 2007). Ethos emphasizes the politician's credibility and trustworthiness. Logos refers to logic-based appeals, often using facts and figures. Messages that contain logos usually appeal to critical voters who aim to understand the logic behind candidates' platforms and policies. Pathos relates to messages that aim to appeal to audience's emotions and sways listeners by triggering feelings of fear, anger, and contempt (often through the use of humor, cynicism, or empathy).[9] In our analysis, the rhetoric was assessed in terms of authoritative voice (ethos), fact-based appeals (logos), and emotional language (pathos) - we examined whether politicians emphasized their skills, used facts, or presented emotions in their posts. While coding the posts, the coders were asked to identify whether each of those rhetoric strategies were used (marking it as 1) or not (marking it as 0).[10] In addition, we examined the topics of the posts in order to learn more about the politicians' messages. The topics examined were security, welfare, economy, call for action (regarding the elections), periphery, personal issues, presenting the politician, attacking opponents, and other topics. The content analysis of the posts was conducted by two trained students using a coding sheet. A reliability test based on a random sample of 15% of the posts ($N = 52$) showed high levels of agreement between the coders (Krippendorf's alpha coefficient no lower than .848).

Results

In line with our study's goal, the results section will examine the amount of users' engagement male and female politicians had generated on social media during an election campaign. But first, we had examined whether the traditional media provide male politicians a better opportunity to present themselves to the public, as suggested by previous studies (Basow, 2016; Braden, 1996; Bystrom et al., 2001; Everitt et al., 2016). In order to do so, we had retrieved the information about the politicians' online traditional media appearances. As aforesaid 11,648 articles dealing with the politicians we had used in our analysis were published during the week leading to the elections and on Election Day (the time frame of our analysis): 9263 dealt with the 19 male politicians examined in the study, while only 2385 had dealt with the 14 female politicians.

Table 2. Differences in online traditional media appearances and in the number of posts published of the politicians' Facebook pages between male and female politicians.

Variables	Gender of politician	*N*	*M*	SD	*T*
Number of articles the politicians appeared on (traditional media)	Males	19	487.53	576.19	2.131*
	Females	14	170.36	255.73	
Number of posts published of the politicians' Facebook page	Males	17	17.94	16.28	0.567
	Females	13	15.15	7.84	

$^{*}P < 0.5$.

Table 2 presents a *T* test examining the salience of male and female politicians in the online traditional media and the number of posts published by male and female politicians during the week leading to Election Day – a topic we deal with below.

As expected, and in line with the existing literature in the field (Basow, 2016; Braden, 1996; Bystrom et al., 2001; Everitt et al., 2016), during the 2015 election campaign, male politicians' media appearance was significantly more salient ($m = 487.53$) than those of female politicians ($m = 170.36$). Our goal was to examine whether those differences also exist on social media, or is it a more equalizing platform for female politicians. In order to examine our research question, we will begin by examining the differences in user engagement generated by male versus female politicians' posts, followed by a multilevel analysis that will examine those differences while controlling for other variables that may have impacted users' engagement.

In terms of differences in the number of posts published by male and female politicians, the findings (Table 2) indicate that there are no significant differences. If so, male and female politicians published a similar amount of posts during the week leading to Election Day. The evidence suggests that any differences in the amount of users' engagement to male and female politicians' posts are not influenced by the number of posts published by the politicians (the number of posts will serve as one of the control variables in the multivariate analysis below).

Differences in users' engagement (as measured by the number of Likes, Shares, comments, and participants) between male and female politicians' posts on Facebook are presented in Table 3.

Our findings indicate that in two of the users' engagement measurements, female politicians' posts generated significantly more engagement in comparison to those of the male politicians; female politicians received more Likes ($m = 2496.40$) and more Shares ($m = 243.47$) compared to male politicians ($m = 1566.53$ for Likes, and $m = 129.23$ for Shares). Surprisingly, the findings indicate that the female politicians tended to generate more engagement among Facebook users (in terms of Likes and Shares) in comparison to male politicians. Thus, in terms of Likes and Shares, social media not only creates an equal ground for female politicians but also enables them to generate more engagement, compared to male politicians. With regard to our third engagement measurement - the number of comments and participants in discussions, no significant differences were found between male and female politicians in the amount of participants in discussions in their Facebook posts. This suggests that with regard to online discussions with politicians, social media provides equal opportunities for politicians to mobilize the public, regardless of their gender.

Table 3. Differences in audience engagement between male and female politicians' posts.

Variables	Gender of politician (posts by)	*N*	*M*	SD	*T*
Likes	Males	305	1566.53	2428.79	3.895***
	Females	196	2496.4	2716.54	
Shares	Males	305	129.23	191.49	2.873**
	Females	196	243.47	535.18	
Comments	Males	305	138.57	286.72	1.246
	Females	196	172.39	311.18	
Participants	Males	305	113.53	242.36	1.272
	Females	196	142.84	257.44	

*$P < .05$; **$P < .01$; ***$P < .001$.

Next, we wanted to see whether those differences still exist while controlling for other variables that may impact users' engagement, in addition to the politicians' gender. Some of those variables are at the politician level, such as the politician's age, party, ranking in the Party's list, and the number of posts the politician had published during the week leading to Election Day; while others are at the post level, including how many days before the elections the post was published and the users' engagement generated. Due to the nature of our data, different posts published by each politician, we used multilevel analysis (using an SPSS mixed model) to examine differences in the engagement male and female politicians' posts generated, while controlling for the remainder of the variables in the model. The findings are presented in Table 4.

As presented in Table 4, the impact of politicians' gender on users' engagement remained significant for both Likes (model 1) and Shares (model 2), while controlling for factors such as the politicians' age, party, ranking in the Party, the number of posts published by the politician, and how many days before the elections the post was published. The findings indicate that even while controlling for other factors, female politicians generated more engagement, in terms of Likes and Shares, in comparison with male politicians, similar to the findings presented in Table 3. As for the number of comments and participants (models 3 and 4), similar to the findings presented in Table 3, no significant differences were found between the number of comments and participants in male and female politicians' post discussions. This indicates that male and female politicians generate a similar amount of comments and participation in their social media discussions. Other factor that were found to have an impact on the level of engagement a post had received were: ranking in the party, for both Likes (model 1) and Shares (model 2), where politicians who were ranked higher in their party generated more user engagement than those lower down the rankings. As for the number of posts published by politicians,

Table 4. Multilevel models predicting audience engagement with politicians' posts of Facebook.

	Model 1: Likes	Model 2: Shares	Model 3: Comments	Model 4: Participants
Fixed effects				
Gender (male = 1)	−1070.93**	−139.41*	−43.78	−35.68
Politician's ranking	−179.09*	−27.83*	−13.12	−10.35
Politician's age	−14.68	−1.43	−.72	−.78
Number of posts	42.99*	2.39	4.26*	3.46*
Days to elections	−165.53***	8.96	−3.51	−4.57
Party 1 – the Likud	2055.76	223.90	269.84	217.13
Party 2 – Israel Bytenu	−1349.53	−52.56	−73.63	−80.15
Party 3 – the Jewish Home	−976.51	8.13	−128.56	−129.50
Party 4 – the Joined List	−805.08	6.76	−19.10	−36.99
Party 5 – Meretz	−509.22	100.01	8.71	−17.24
Party 6 – the Zionist Camp (Labor)	163.03	198.21	42.80	14.05
Party 7 – Yesh Atid	−1565.71	−54.38	−38.98	−49.09
Party 8 – Kulanu	−169.48	90.61	41.29	22.84
Party 9 – Shas	0.00	0.00	0.00	0.00
Intercept	2733.54	121.41	116.90	132.26
Variance of random components				
Politician	4,951,632.09***	121,347.92***	73,875.93***	52,147.98***
−2 Restricted log likelihood	8973.48	7168.69	6803.16	6757.67
N	501	501	501	501

Note: The statistical procedure is multilevel (hierarchical) model (using SPSS MIXED model). The variance type is variance component. SPSS uses the restricted maximum likelihood (REML) method for mix model analysis. Entries are parameter estimates.

***$P < .001$, **$P < .01$, *$P < .05$

the higher the number of posts published by a politician, the higher the number of Likes (model 1), comments (model 3), and participants (model 4) his/her posts had generated. In terms of post timing, it appears that users tended to Like politicians' posts more as the elections drew closer (model 1).

Thus, our findings reveal that social media provides a supportive environment for female politicians; female politicians generated the same number of comments and participants as male politicians did in terms of responses to their posts. Beyond our expectation that social media provides a more equal environment for female politicians, our findings in fact indicate that in terms of Likes and Shares, female politicians tended to generate more users' engagement than male politicians did. The evidence suggests that social media provides female politicians with an opportunity to mobilize their public and may assist them in promoting themselves during election campaigns.

Next, in order to obtain a wider perspective on those findings, the analysis turns to examine the content of the politicians' posts - that is, their rhetoric and the topics discussed. Our hypothesis suggested that in today's 'double-voiced' political context, there are no differences in the rhetoric used and topics discussed by male versus female politicians. In terms of rhetoric, in line with H1, no significant differences were found between male and female politicians in terms of voice (ethos),[11] fact-based appeals (logos),[12] and emotional language (Pathos).[13] The evidence thus suggests (in accordance with H1) that the rhetoric of male versus female politicians is similar, with both using authoritative voice, facts, and emotions in their messages. With respect to the topics discussed by the politicians, Table 5 presents the correlation between politicians' gender and the topic discussed in the post.

The most frequent aspect discussed in the politicians' posts during the election campaign involved presenting themselves to the public; however, as the findings exhibit (Table 5), this was a more salient topic for the females (53.3% of the posts) than for the males (39.4%). It appears that politicians in general, and women in particular, take advantage of the social media platform to expose details about themselves to potential voters. A

Table 5. The topics raised by male and female politicians in the posts.

Topics		Male	Female	Total
Personal issues	Count	14	18	32
	% within gender	10.60%	10.80%	10.70%
Security	Count	9	6	15
	% within gender	6.80%	3.60%	5.00%
Presenting the politician	Count	52	89	141
	% within gender	39.40%	53.30%	47.20%
Economy	Count	4	1	5
	% within gender	3.00%	0.60%	1.70%
Call for action (elections)	Count	15	4	19
	% within gender	11.40%	2.40%	6.40%
Periphery	Count	4	7	11
	% within gender	3.00%	4.20%	3.70%
Welfare	Count	6	4	10
	% within gender	4.50%	2.40%	3.30%
Attacking the opponents	Count	14	34	48
	% within gender	10.60%	20.40%	16.10%
Other topics	Count	14	4	18
	% within gender	10.60%	2.40%	6.00%
Total	Count	132	167	299

Note: χ^2 (8) = 30.404, Rc = 0.319, $P < .001$.

more surprising result relates to the usage of this platform for attacking opponents - in contrast to female stereotypes as soft and less confrontational than men, they used their posts for such attacks 20.4% more than male politicians did (10.6%). Male politicians used their posts in attempts to mobilize the public, as 'call for action' (with regard to the elections) was a more salient topic in their messages (11.4%, in comparison to only 2.4% of female posts). Security issues were also more salient in the male politicians' posts (6.8%, in comparison to 3.6% for female posts), as were discussions about the economy (3% of male politicians' posts vs. 0.6% of females' posts) and welfare (4.5% of male politicians' posts vs. 2.4% of females' posts). Interestingly, representation of the politicians' personal issues (their private lives, families, etc.) was similar for male (10.6%) and female (10.8%) politicians. Another interesting finding pertains to the representation of gender as part of the election campaign; 21% of the messages posted by female politicians dealt with gender issues - in their posts, women emphasized 'girl power', the importance of having women in salient positions in politics, and the need to mobilize women to support them.

In accordance with H1, the examination of politicians' rhetoric on social media did not reveal gender differences in their usage of authoritative voice, facts, and emotions in their messages; however, analysis of the topics did suggest differences in the issues raised by male versus female politicians – for example, female politicians tend to present themselves and attack their opponents more than male politicians who try to mobilize their supporters more than female politicians in their social media posts.

Conclusions

This study aimed to examine whether social media provides a more equal opportunity for female politicians, in terms of generating user engagement and mobilizing supporters. Based on past studies (supported by results presented in the current analysis), which have revealed that in the traditional media male politicians usually receive more salient coverage (Basow, 2016; Braden, 1996; Bystrom et al., 2001; Everitt et al., 2016), as well as recent study findings that social networks serve as a more supportive environment for women, compared to men (Joiner et al., 2016; Wang et al., 2013), our study focused on male versus female politicians' ability to promote themselves by engaging social media users during an election campaign, using the Israeli 2015 elections as our case study. Beyond our expectations that social media provides a more equal environment for female politicians, our findings in fact indicate that social media enables female politicians to generate *more* engagement; their posts generated significantly more user engagement in terms of the number of Likes and Shares they received in comparison to male politicians, while they had the same number of comments and participants in discussions. These results were found to remain significant while controlling for other factors, such as the politician's age, party, and ranking; the number of posts the politician had published during the week leading to Election Day; and the timing of the posts (how many days before Election Day they were posted). The evidence shows that social media serves as a better and fairer tool in promoting female politicians. Our findings correspond with those of previous studies in the field, suggesting that women gain more support than men on social media (Joiner et al., 2014, 2016; Wang et al., 2013), and that this particularly applies to female politicians (as found in McGregor and Mourão's (2016) study focusing on Twitter). In line with recent findings that the popularity of the 'double-voiced' discourse politicians tend to use, presenting the stereotypically male authoritative voice alongside stereotypically female emotional language (Cameron & Shaw, 2016; Kenty, 2016), our findings did not exhibit differences in the rhetoric used by male versus female politicians in their social media posts, but did suggest differences in the issues raised by male versus female politicians.

A possible explanation for female politicians' ability to generate more public engagement compared to males could be that in order to succeed in the masculine political sphere, female leaders have to be extremely talented and charismatic (Alessio & Andrzejewski, 2000; Davies-Netzley, 1998). The social media environment, which enables individuals to directly communicate with a wide range of audiences without relying on the editing of traditional media (which has been found to be less supportive of female politicians), enables them to move forward by exposing details about themselves in a manner that allows them to receive the public's support.

These findings suggest an optimistic view for the future in terms of representation of women in politics, and their ability to attract more attention and mobilize their supporters via social media, which now serves as a main stage for political campaigning and deliberation. This is particularly important as studies have found that media attention during an election campaign is crucial for politicians' electoral success (Harrop, 1987; van Aelst, Maddens, Noppe, & Fiers, 2008). Both traditional media (Sheafer & Weimann, 2005; van Aelst et al., 2008) and digital media, especially in the form of social networks (Gibson & McAllister, 2006; Suddulich & Wall, 2010; Yarchi et al., 2017), has been found to contribute to the electoral success of parties and candidates. Thus, female politicians' ability to better engage with social media users and mobilize their supporters can improve their electoral success, and may even lead to a more equal representation of women in politics.

Future studies should continue to examine the advantages of social media for female politicians in other political contexts and countries, and based on other social networking platforms. If our findings are mirrored in such analyses, the long-lasting notion regarding female politicians' media inferiority would be challenged, illustrating that in our contemporary media environment, where online social networking sites serve as a central campaigning tool and public political deliberation stage, female politicians may even have an advantage over their male peers. A main limitation of the study is the short time frame of the analysis and future studies should try to examine the gender factors examined here also during the routine. Another limitation is that analysis of all the 120 Israeli parliament member candidates, which was beyond the resources of our current study, would have provided a wider perspective of the gender differences.

Notes

1. It is important to note that Twitter is not a popular social network in Israel, with Twitter active users forming a mere 0.5% of Facebook users in Israel (Mor, 2016).
2. In the 1999 and 2001 election campaigns, the electoral system was changed to a 'direct election of the prime minister' system. Citizens were given two ballots and asked to vote for a particular candidate for prime minister, and a political party for the Knesset. In the 2003 elections, Israel returned to the original system.
3. The only female politician who did not get a matching male politician in our study was Shelly Yachimovich – ranked third in the Zionist Camp, since the politicians ranked second and fourth on the party's list were also female.

4. A recent study examining the normalization hypothesis on social media during the Israeli 2015 election campaign had found that Prime Minister Netanyahu had a significant advantage in his social media campaign (Lev-On & Haleva-Amir, 2018).
5. A total of 196 posts were published by the 14 female politicians examined, and 305 by the 19 male politicians sampled in our study.
6. Yaakov Litzman (the head of Yahadut Hatora - an ultra-orthodox party) and Abd Al Hakeem Haj Yahya (from the Joined List party) are two of the only few Knesset members who does not have a Facebook account. For Litzman, a possible explanation for not using social media could be the fact that his voters and supporters are less likely to use those platforms, due to religious reasons. Rachel Azaria (a new Knesset member for Kulanu) had opened a Facebook page after she was elected to serve as a Knesset member.
7. We also controlled for this factor in our politician sampling.
8. For this part of the analysis, we used all available posts from our original sample.
9. Posts using terms associated with emotions (such as fear, joy, anger) as well as writing which reflects emotional attitudes (such as hostility, aggression, optimism) were coded as using pathos.
10. A post could contain more than one rhetoric strategy.
11. [$T_{(297)} = -1.423$; *NS*]
12. [$T_{(297)} = 0.570$; *NS*]
13. [$T_{(296)} = 1.129$; *NS*]

Disclosure statement

No potential conflict of interest was reported by the authors.

Notes on contributors

Moran Yarchi Ph.D. is a Senior Lecturer at the Sammy Ofer School of Communications, and the Co-Head of the Public Diplomacy program, at the Interdisciplinary Center (IDC) Herzliya, Israel. Her main area of research is political communication, especially the media's coverage of conflicts and public diplomacy [email: moran.yarchi@gmail.com].

Tal Samuel-Azran (PhD, University of Melbourne; MA, New York University) is the Head of the international program at the Sammy Ofer School of Communications. His main fields of research are political communication, new media, public diplomacy and media globalization [email: azrant7@gmail.com].

ORCID

Moran Yarchi http://orcid.org/0000-0002-8044-2145

References

Aday, S., & Devitt, J. (2001). Style over substance: Newspaper coverage of Elizabeth Dole's presidential bid. *The International Journal of Press/Politics*, *6*(2), 52–73.

Alessio, J., & Andrzejewski, J. (2000). Unveiling the glass ceiling: An analysis of the cohort claim effect. *American Sociological Review*, *65*(2), 311–315.

Alexa. (2016). Top 500 Global Sites. Retrieved from http://www.alexa.com/topsites

Andersen, K. (1996). *After suffrage: Women in partisan and electoral politics before the New Deal.* Chicago, IL: University of Chicago Press.

Armento-Cota, J. (2011). Multiple perspectives on the influence of gender in online interactions. *Sociology Compass*, *5*(1), 23–36.

Balmas, M., Rahat, G., Sheafer, T., & Shenhav, S. R. (2014). Two routes to personalized politics centralized and decentralized personalization. *Party Politics, 20*(1), 37–51.
Basow, S. A. (2016). Evaluation of female leaders: Stereotypes, prejudice, and discrimination. In M. E. Paludi (Ed.), *Why Congress need women* (pp. 85–100). Santa Barbara, CA: Preager.
Bass, B. (1998). *Transformational leadership: Industrial, military and educational impact.* Mahwah, NJ: Erlbaum.
Baxter, J. (2011). Survival or success? A critical exploration of the use of "double-voiced discourse" by women businessleaders in the UK. *Discourse and Language, 5*(3), 231–245.
Braden, M. (1996). *Women, politics and the media.* Lexington, KE: University Press of Kentucky.
Brandtzaeg, P. B. (2015). Facebook is no "great equalizer": A big data approach to gender differences in civic engagement across countries. *Social Science Computer Review, 35*(1), 103–125.
Brescoll, V. L. (2016). Leading with their hearts? How gender stereotypes of emotion lead to biased evaluations of female leaders. *The Leadership Quarterly, 27*(3), 415–428.
Bronstein, J. (2013). Like me! Analyzing the 2012 presidential candidates' Facebook pages. *Online Information Review, 37*(2), 173–192.
Bystrom, D. G., Robertson, T. A., & Banwart, M. C. (2001). Framing the fight: An analysis of media coverage of female and male candidates in primary races for governor and US Senate in 2000. *American Behavioral Scientist, 44*(12), 1999–2013.
Cameron, D. (2006). Theorising the female voice in public contexts. In J. Baxter (Ed.), *Speaking out in public contexts* (pp. 3–20). Basingstoke: Palgrave.
Cameron, D., & Shaw, S. (2016). Gender and speech styles in the 2015 general election debates. In D. Cameron, & S. Shaw (Eds.), *Gender, power and political speech: Women and language in the 2015 UK general election* (pp. 27–78). New York, NY: Springer.
Davies-Netzley, S. (1998). Women above the glass ceiling: Perceptions on corporate mobility and strategies for success. *Gender & Society, 12*(3), 339–355.
Erikson, E. (2008). Hillary is my friend: MySpace and political fandom. *Rocky Mountain Communication Review, 4*(2), 3–16.
Everitt, J., Best, L. A., & Gaudet, D. (2016). Candidate gender, behavioral style, and willingness to vote. *American Behavioral Scientist, 60*(14), 1737–1755.
Gibson, R. K., & McAllister, I. (2006). Does cyber-campaigning win votes? Online communication in the 2004 Australian election. *Journal of Elections, Public Opinion & Parties, 16*(3), 243–263.
Gidengil, E., & Everitt, J. (1999). Metaphors and misrepresentation: Gendered mediation in news coverage of the 1993 Canadian leaders' debates. *The International Journal of Press/Politics, 4* (1), 48–65.
Gilligan, C. (1982). *In a different voice.* Cambridge, MA: Harvard University Press.
Golden, J. L., Berquist, G. F., Coleman, W. E., Golden, R., & Sproule, J. M. (Eds.). (2007). *The rhetoric of western thought: From the Mediterranean world to the global setting* (9th ed.). Dubuque, IA: Kendall Hunt.
Haleva-Amir, S. (2011). Online Israeli politics: Current state of the art. *Israel Affairs, 17*(3), 467–485.
Harrop, M. (1987). Voters. In J. Seaton & B. Pimlott (Eds.), *The media in British politics* (pp. 45–63). Aldershot: Dartmouth.
Hayat, T., Lesser, O., & Samuel-Azran, T. (2017). Gendered discourse patterns on online social networks: A social network analysis perspective. *Computers in Human Behavior, 77,* 132–139.
Hayes, D., & Lawless, J. L. (2015). A non-gendered lens? Media, voters, and female candidates in contemporary congressional elections. *Perspectives on Politics, 13*(1), 95–118.
Hayes, D., Lawless, J. L., & Baltinger, G. (2014). Who cares what they wear? Media, gender, and the influence of candidate appearance. *Social Science Quarterly, 95*(5), 1194–1212.
Herzog, H. (1998). More than a looking glass: Women in Israeli local politics and the media. *The International Journal of Press/Politics, 3*(1), 26–47.
Hooghe, M., Jacobs, M., & Claes, E. (2015). Enduring gender bias in reporting on political elite positions: Media coverage of female MPs in Belgian news broadcasts (2003–2011). *The International Journal of Press/Politics, 20*(4), 395–414.

Joiner, R., Stewart, C., Beaney, C., Moon, A., Maras, P., Guiller, J., … Brosnan, M. (2014). Publically different, privately the same: Gender differences and similarities in response to Facebook status updates. *Computers in Human Behavior*, *39*, 165–169.

Joiner, R., Cuprinskaite, J., Dapkeviciute, L., Johnson, H., Gavin, J., & Brosnan, M. (2016). Gender differences in response to Facebook status updates from same and opposite gender friends. *Computers in Human Behavior*, *58*, 407–412.

Kabir, M., & Urbach, A. (2013, May). Facebook exposes: How many Israelis are surfing the social network? *Calcalist* (in Hebrew). Retrieved from http://www.calcalist.co.il/internet/articles/0,7340,L-3602989,00.html

Kenty, J. (2016, August 22). Hillary Clinton's rhetorical persona. *Eidolon*. Retrieved from https://eidolon.pub/hillary-clintons-rhetorical-persona-9af06a3c4b03#.5xie87w0p

Koc-Michalska, K., Gibson, R., & Vedel, T. (2014). Online campaigning in France, 2007–2012: Political actors and citizens in the aftermath of the Web.2.0 evolution. *Journal of Information Technology and Politics*, *11*(2), 220–244.

Koller, V. (2004). Businesswomen and war metaphors: Possessive, jealous and pugnacious? *Journal of Sociolinguistics*, *8*(1), 3–22.

Lakoff, R. (1975). *Language and woman's place*. New York, NY: Harper and Row.

Lev-On, A., & Haleva-Amir, S. (2018). Normalizing or equalizing? Characterizing Facebook campaigning. *New Media and Society*, *20*(2), 720–739.

Livak, L., Lev-On, A., & Doron, G. (2011). MK websites and the personalization of Israeli politics. *Israel Affairs*, *17*(3), 445–466.

Malhotra, A., Malhotra, C. K., & See, A. (2013). How to create brand engagement on Facebook. *MIT Sloan Management Review*, *54*(2), 1–4.

McElhinny, B. (1995). Challenging hegemonic masculinities: Female and male police officers handling domestic violence. In K. Hall & M. Bucholtz (Eds.), *Gender articulated: Language and the socially constructed self* (pp. 217–243). New York, NY: Routledge.

McGregor, S. C., & Mourão, R. R. (2016). Talking politics on Twitter: Gender, elections, and social networks. *Social Media + Society*.

Metzgar, E., & Maruggi, A. (2009). Social media and the 2008 US presidential election. *Journal of New Communications Research*, *4*(1), 141–165.

Mills, S. (2006). Gender and performance anxiety at academic conferences. In J. Baxter (Ed.), *Speaking out in public contexts* (pp. 61–80). Basingstoke: Palgrave.

Mor, Y. (2016, October 7). The Twitter lie: Half of Twitter accounts in Israel are fake. *Mako*. Retrieved from http://www.mako.co.il/nexter-magazine/Article-18348767ba72751006.htm

Patti, M., Valkenburg, J. P., & Schouten, A. P. (2006). Friend networking sites and their relationship to adolescents' well-being and social self-esteem. *CyberPsychology & Behavior*, *9*(5), 584–590.

Peer, H. (2016, December). Why do women use social networks so effectively. *Davar Rishon* (in Hebrew). Retrieved from http://www.davar1.co.il/44070/

Priola, C., & Brannen, M. J. (2009). "Between a rock and a hard place": Exploring women's experiences of participation and progress in managerial careers. *Equal Opportunities International*, *28*(5), 378–397.

Ross, K., Evans, E., Harrison, L., Shears, M., & Wadia, K. (2013). The gender of news and news of gender: A study of sex, politics, and press coverage of the 2010 British general election. *The International Journal of Press/Politics*, *18*(1), 3–20.

Samuel-Azran, T., Yarchi, M., & Wolfsfeld, G. (2015). Aristotelian rhetoric and Facebook success in Israel's 2013 election campaign. *Online Information Review*, *39*(2), 149–162.

Samuel-Azran, T., Yarchi, M., & Wolfsfeld, G. (2016). Rhetoric styles and political affiliations during Israel's 2013 "Facebook elections. *International Journal of Politics, Culture, and Society*.

Schnurr, S. (2009). *Leadership discourse at work: Interactions of humour, gender and workplace culture*. Basingstoke: Palgrave.

Shaw, S. (2000). Language, gender and floor apportionment in political debates. *Discourse & Society*, *11*(3), 401–418.

Sheafer, T., & Weimann, G. (2005). Agenda building, agenda setting, priming, individual voting intentions, and the aggregate results: An analysis of four Israeli elections. *Journal of Communication*, *55*(2), 347–365.

Sinclair, A. (1998). *Doing leadership differently. Gender, power and sexuality in a changing business culture*. Melbourne: Melbourne University Press.

Suddulich, M., & Wall, M. (2010). Cyber campaigning in the 2007 Irish general election. *Journal of Information Technology and Politics*, *7*(4), 340–355.

UN Women. (2017). Facts and figures: Leadership and political participation. Retrieved from http://www.unwomen.org/en/what-we-do/leadership-and-political-participation/facts-and-figures

van Aelst, P., Maddens, B., Noppe, J., & Fiers, S. (2008). Politicians in the news: Media or party logic? Media attention and electoral success in the Belgian election campaign of 2003. *European Journal of Communication*, *2*(2), 193–210.

Vromen, A., Xenos, M. A., & Loader, B. (2015). Young people, social media and connective action: From organizational maintenance to everyday political talk. *Journal of Youth Studies*, *18*(1), 80–100.

Walsh, C. (2001). *Gender and discourse: Language and power in politics, the church and organizations*. London: Longman.

Wang, Y. C., Burke, M., & Kraut, R. E. (2013, April). Gender, topic, and audience response: an analysis of user-generated content on Facebook. In *Proceedings of the SIGCHI Conference on Human Factors in Computing System* (pp. 31–34). Paris: SIGCHI society.

Wasburn, P. C., & Wasburn, M. H. (2011). Media coverage of women in politics: The curious case of Sarah Palin. *Media, Culture & Society*, *33*(7), 1027–1041.

Wodak, R. (1997). "I know we won't revolutionise the world with this, but …": Styles of female leadership in institutions. In H. Kotthoff & R. Wodak (Eds.), *Communicating Gender in Context (Pragmatics and Beyond, New Series)* (pp. 335–370). Amsterdam: John Benjamins.

Wolfsfeld, G., Yarchi, M., & Samuel-Azran, T. (2016). Political information repertoires and political participation. *New Media & Society*, *18*(9), 2096–2115.

Yarchi, M., Wolfsfeld, G., Samuel-Azran, T., & Segev, E. (2017). Invest, engage, and win: Online election campaigns and their outcomes in an Israeli election. In M. Brown (Ed.), *Social media performance evaluation and success measurements* (pp. 225–248). Hershey, PA: IGI Global.

5 Commitment in the cloud? Social media participation in the sunflower movement

Yuan Hsiao and Yunkang Yang

ABSTRACT

Social media participants in digitally enabled protests have long been criticized for their lack of commitment. Many bypassed this issue and argued that social media's positive impact on protests does not require high commitment. We empirically test the lack of commitment claim in the case of the 2014 Sunflower Movement in Taiwan. Using survey data from a sample of 801 participants, we find a group of highly active social media participants – what we described as the 'cloud activists' – who operated exclusively online during the movement. We find that the commitment of the 'cloud activists', in terms of both identification and sense of efficacy, is at least in par with, if not always necessarily higher than, most offline participants. Furthermore, contrasting previous findings on the positive linear relationship between social media use and offline participation, we find the effect of social media can be either positive or negative, depending on the level of social media activity. We suggest that production in virtual space of contentious politics may consist of different processes – peer production by the online crowd and connective leadership by the 'cloud activists' who shoulder extra responsibilities. Identifying 'cloud activists' may help us achieve a better understanding of these two interrelated processes as well as the way in which digitally enabled protests persist and transform over time.

Digital media has brought forth unprecedented opportunities for citizens to autonomously and collectively participate in democracy. Today, many oppositional movements take place in an augmented reality (Jurgenson, 2012) where the power of digitality meets the politics of physicality. From the Taksim Square in Gezi Park protests to the Tahrir Square in the Arab Spring, from Zuccotti Park in the Occupy Movement to central Hong Kong in the Umbrella Movement, protesters have demonstrated the power of flesh-and-blood body politics facilitated and amplified by social media. Social media optimists seem to have successfully defeated the 'slacktivism' argument, but on both sides there is a tendency to treat social media participants as lacking commitment. This widely shared assumption mischaracterizes social media participation in protests (e.g., neglecting highly intensive online organizing activities such as linking, remixing, and curating or sustained online activities such as archiving protest resources that may require high commitment), obfuscates the multilayered roles various social media participants take, and hinders the understanding of the way in which digitally enabled protests persist and transform over time.

Social media critics such as Morozov (2011) and Gladwell (2010) argue that social media participation characterized by decentralization and networked individualism is inconsequential to push forward political changes because successful protest movements require hierarchy, discipline, and centralization. This point of view, based on the traditional model of movement organizing, is refuted by two lines of thought that demonstrate that social media is an important, if not central, aspect of movements. The first line demonstrates how online participation on social media itself contributes to oppositional movements. Bennett and Segerberg (2013) argue that self-motivated sharing practices on social media can enable 'connective action' characteristic of loose coordination and decentralization. Individuals' tiny acts of posting and retweeting, when aggregated, produce a crowd-sourced organizational structure that is able to mobilize resources, respond to external events, and adapt to changes in the long haul (Bennett, Segerberg, & Walker, 2014). Contrary to Morozov's view, connective actions did achieve impressive political gains such as toppling the regime in Egypt and bringing back the long-ignored issue of inequality to the US public sphere (Bennett, 2012). Penney and Dadas (2014) also argued that social media participation can create a networked counter-public that attracts sympathizers and challenges the power of mainstream media. Other works distinguish the unique contributions made by different types of social media users such as initiating information cascade and amplifying message reach.(Barbera et al., 2015; González-Bailón, Borge-Holthoefer, & Moreno, 2013). The second line identifies mechanisms through which social media facilitate offline mobilization such as news consumption (Gil de Zúñiga, Jung, & Valenzuela, 2012), opinion expression (Valenzuela, 2013), framing of online comments (Harlow, 2012), or providing social information that bolsters the estimation of the likelihood of success (Margetts, John, & Yasseri, 2015).

However, the claim that social media participants lack commitment is only half true. This study uses survey data from the Sunflower movement to systemically investigate commitment levels of social media participants and identifies a group of online-only social media participants who are highly committed. We call them 'cloud activists'. 'Cloud', as a metaphor, speaks to the dynamic and distributed nature of the protest space. It designates a virtual space where online networks and discourses constantly grow, interconnect, disjoin, or break down, which may or may not be connected with physical locations of contention. 'Activists', on the other hand, signifies invested and committed core participants, and sets them apart from bystander publics and half-hearted participants in the online crowd. The finding of high commitment among the cloud activists is also validated by a non-linear relationship between social media activity and offline participation, which suggests that committed cloud activists may choose to actualize their commitment online through sustained or highly intensive organizing activities. Our findings of highly committed social media participants and the non-linear relationship between social media activity and offline participation add to our current understanding of social media and protests, as we direct the long-overdue attention to the digitally enabled forms of highly committed participation which may hold the key to understanding how digitally enabled protests persist and transform over time.

Social media participation and commitment

Confronted with evidence on the mechanisms and impact of social media (e.g., Bennett et al., 2014; Gil de Zúñiga et al., 2012), Gladwell (2010) and Morozov (2011) seem to have lost the debate on the consequentialist account. However, the issue of commitment, a crucial part of their criticism against social media participation, has so far been ignored. To them, being on the ground in a protest suggests a high level of commitment because one needs to physically go to a place, face the police, or even risk his/her life; on the other hand, social media participation – clicking a few 'like' buttons or retweeting a few posts – is treated as 'civic promiscuity' or identity shopping (Morozov, 2011) because of the lack of commitment. As Morozov (2011) puts it, social media participation in a protest is not 'deep, meaningful, and spiritual' (p. 184) but cursory and shallow. Morozov (2011) compares political engagement on social media to assembling cultural objects and putting together a version of one's self – 'much of it happens for reasons that have nothing to do with one's commitment to ideas and politics in general, but rather to impress one's friends' (p. 186); Gladwell (2010) relates the lack of commitment to online weak ties that social media tend to afford and suggests that only strong ties can enable high commitment to social causes. In short, they argue that social media participation does not embody personal devotion or persistence observed in previous successful social movements.

Few scholars have engaged the debate with Gladwell and Morozov head-on in terms of the commitment of social media participants. It is understandable that this issue was not central in previous debate. For one thing, both sides recognize the ethos of late modern politics: Gladwell agreed that today's political participation is much different from the way of doing politics in the 1960s and 1970s; Bennett (1998) characterized it as 'lifestyle politics' – fluid political engagement anchored in personal values, self-image, and consumer choice. For another, the power of social media does not depend on deep commitment. It lessens the level of commitment participation required so that the tiny and fitful acts of producing and sharing information here and there can jointly produce organization in the crowd (Bennett et al., 2014).

However, one should not sidestep the question of commitment even when peer production in digitally enabled protests does not presuppose it. Commitment, one of the four components of Tilly's WUNC (worthiness, unity, numbers, and commitment) formula, still matters (2004). As evidenced historically by the African-American civil rights movement and the Indian Independence movement, it is hard to imagine that any protest could achieve any significant political change without having committed activists willing to put in extra hours, prioritize protest activities over their personal life, risk reprisal from companies or governments (McAdam, 1986), or endure adversarial conditions in prolonged struggles (Pfaff, Hechter, & Corcoran, 2016; Taylor, 1989). This is no less true for today's large-scale protests – the *Indignados* movement is survived by its core activists who later formed the left-wing party *Podemos* and secured 21% of the vote in the 2015 election in Spain; the spirit of the Occupy movement is revived by its core online activists such as Winnie Wong who later formed grass root campaigns such as People for Bernie. This suggests that there exist such highly committed social media activists that may have played an indispensable role in archiving and preserving protest resources in times of decline, adapting the movement to changing political environment, or passing on their lessons to other movements. Ignoring highly committed social media activists misses the important work they do and hinders our understanding of how a movement adapts, morphs, or declines in the digital age.

Unfortunately, despite its importance, the issue of commitment has seldom been addressed with social media participation. Many impose the stamp of lack of commitment onto all social media participants and argue that only offline participation signals strong commitment. According to Morozov, being an information hub that produces, curates, and disseminates information in a protest does not make one a committed dissident – only involvement in offline risky behavior does. This point of view, which posits that only those offline participants are committed to the cause, could not be echoed more starkly by Kavada (2015). Calling social media participants online spectators, Kavada argued that social media only assumes a supportive role in terms of diffusing protest messages and sustaining the commitment of offline participants. 'For the activists on the ground, online spectators and their message of solidarity were important for sustaining their commitment to the movement for helping them to weather the difficult conditions of the physical occupation' (Kavada, 2015, p. 880). Social media users are consigned to the outer ring whereas it is the inner ring offline participants that constitute the collectives of the occupy movement (Kavada, 2015). This dichotomy between committed offline participants and half-hearted online participants is also reflected in Karpf's comments about membership in the Occupy movement as being determined by physically showing up (2014).

The reason why only offline participants can possibly be credited with commitment is largely because previous scholars understand commitment only in terms of bearing personal cost of risky offline behavior such as civil disobedience. However, online-only participation can also entail a great amount of risk and demand a high level of personal sacrifice and devotion. Online participation can be risky in countries where surveillance is widely employed to monitor the behavior of citizens.

For example, online participation in the protests against mining projects in Colombia demands high levels of commitment because many fear that the mining companies would retaliate once the digital trace of resistance is uncovered (Specht & Ros-Tonen, 2016). Even in countries that are less oppressive, continued online participation that takes up a tremendous amount of time from an individual's personal life also suggest deep commitment. Bastos and Mercea (2016) found continued participation by transnational veteran activists who posted profusely in multiple geographically disparate protests over a long period of time and argued that this type of online work can never be done by uncommitted, half-hearted, or short burst activists. Therefore, to argue that all online participants are less committed than offline participants is a misleading over-generalization. Not all social media participants are spectators. Different levels of social media participation are common in many movements (see Bennett et al., 2014; Della Ratta & Valeriani, 2014; Morell, 2012; Zhou & Yang, 2017). This could suggest different levels of commitment. An empirical test of commitment not only addresses this long-neglected issue, but also sheds light upon important questions on long-term gains of collective action, such as whether cumulative achievements can be made through online participation collectively. For instance, they could provide the emotional and infrastructural support for offline participants or transfer previous online resources to new protests.

Measuring commitment: identification and efficacy

Commitment may take on various forms: to some, commitment is shown in terms of duration – persistent involvement in the social cause; to others, commitment is manifested in terms of intensity – personal sacrifice or prioritization of activities in the social cause. For Freelon, McIlwain, and Clark (2016), committed online participation in Black Lives Matter movement is manifested as tweeting at least once in three days. For Pfaff et al. (2016), commitment is treated as the endurance of threatening conditions. Committed individuals may vary in the way in which they commit to a social cause, but they share the common root of commitment – psychological investment in a collective cause (Porter, Crampon, & Smith, 1976; Robertson & Tang, 1995). In social movement studies, identification and efficacy have been established as two crucial psychological factors of commitment (Finkel, Muller, & Opp, 1989; Klandermans, 2002; van Zomeren, Postmes, & Spears, 2008). Social identity refers to how the individual self is derived from a collective group (Klandermans & de Weerd, 2000; Tajfel & Turner, 1979) while efficacy originates from Bandura's measurement on the extent of one's belief in one's own ability to complete goals (1982) and has been used in social movement research in reference to the individual's perceived conception that political conditions can be changed through protest (Gamson, 1992).

The framework of psychological factors enables us to distinguish the committed from the lax without imposing a specific form that commitment takes on. Those who are psychologically invested are more likely to make personal sacrifice, bear extra cost, or plod through prolonged struggles. Klandermans and de Weerd's (2000) study on the linkage between identification and intention suggest that committed individuals anticipate protesting in the future. Saunders, Grasso, Olcese, Rainsford, and Rootes (2012) show that repeated participants in European demonstrations have higher levels of identification compared to novices or returners. Finally, a recent study on the Occupy Movement in the US reveals that identification and efficacy predict willingness on participation in the movement even when costly conditions are implicated (Morgan & Chan, 2016). In short, commitment as embodied in identification and efficacy, provide the psychological roots for various forms of manifestations, such as willingness to bear extra costs or engage in repeated participation.

Hypotheses

Driven by Gladwell (2010) and Morozov's (2011) critique, we first test the hypothesis (H1) that online-only participants are on average less committed than offline participants. However, as implied by studies that suggest non-trivial psychological investment by online activists (e.g., Bastos & Mercea, 2016), we test the hypothesis (H2) that online-only participants with high social media activity as related to the protest have comparable commitment than offline participants. Third, we revisit the conventional wisdom that social media help mobilize offline participation. Under certain conditions, a positive relationship between social media use and offline protest participation has been found (Harlow, 2012; Valenzuela, 2013). Tufekci and Wilson (2012) examined whether social media use has an effect on offline participation in Tahrir Square on the first day only; Valenzuela (2013) lumped different types of protest behavior together (e.g., attending debates and signing a petition) in his analysis without focusing on offline protest participation; Harlow

(2012) examined the effect of Facebook use on protest participation without taking into account of other social media use. However, if our H2 holds water, it then implies that people that are most active on social media may choose not to participate offline. Hence, the mobilizing effect of social media use may not apply to the most active social media participants. Therefore, we test the hypothesis (H3) that there is a positive relationship between protest-related social media activity and offline protest participation.

Method

Case description

We select the Sunflower Movement to test our hypotheses. The Sunflower Movement was driven by students and civic groups in the capital city of Taiwan between 18 March and 10 April 2014. Participants protested the passing of the Cross-Strait Service Trade Agreement because it was passed without clause-by-clause legislative review. Protestors occupied the parliament for 20 days, and on 30 March the protest rallied over half a million participants in a public demonstration (Ho, 2015), marking it the largest event organized by Taiwanese students.

The Sunflower Movement is selected for multiple reasons. First, it is suitable to study the notion of commitment. Protestors that occupied the parliament did risk legal prosecution from the government for quite a long time (Ho, 2015). Compared to one-day demonstrations, long-term occupation such as the Sunflower Movement requires activists to devote energy to continued mobilization, interactions with mainstream media, and negotiations with politicians. Secondly, it generated high visibility on social media, as the official Facebook page received more than 390,000 likes. During the Sunflower Movement, activists constantly solicited suggestions for protest goals and requested for resources on social media, suggesting that devotion occurred not only in the physical site but perhaps online as well. Also, as the internet penetration rate of those between ages 18–30 is 100% (Taiwan Network Information Center, 2014), selection bias regarding internet usage is considerably small. Finally, Taiwan is a democratic state with limited Internet censorship, which may generalize better to protests with similar societal conditions, such as Occupy or Black Lives Matter.

Numerous scholars have investigated social media use in the Sunflower Movement. For example, Chen, Ping, and Chen (2015) found that social media in the Sunflower movement provides a platform for online expression of negative emotions that promotes various forms of political participation; Rowen (2015) documented that online tech-savvy activists who advocated flat organization also engaged in offline organizing activities (e.g., set up video cameras to support live feeds online); Xing and Jin (2014) documented the way in which online participants used Facebook to publicize offline events. Based on anecdotal evidence, most of the previous studies aforementioned emphasized the important role of social media participants in the movement and suggested multilayered roles of online participants. We add to the existing knowledge about the movement by systemically investigating the specific issue of the mobilization effect of social media in the movement – whether social media use mobilized online participants to participate offline, and differentiating various forms online participation based on psychological commitment.

Survey design and implementation

This study utilizes an online questionnaire that contains 50 questions on basic demographics such as age, income, gender, psychological states before and during the movement, participation in the movement, and past political and protest experience. The questionnaire was posted online on PTT, a large forum site in Taiwan (see next section), from 5 May 2015 to 25 June 2015.

The questionnaire is in Mandarin Chinese (Taiwan's official language). It consists of around 50 mandatory questions (varying due to skip patterns) and takes about 10–15 minutes to complete. The questionnaire is a retrospective survey that asks about respondents' behavior and thoughts. It was composed of sections including basic demographics, media use patterns before and during the movement, psychological states before and during the movement, participation in the movement, and past political and protest experience.

To reduce the problem of endogeneity between variables, the questionnaire draws upon life history techniques (Berney & Blane, 1997; Freedman, Thornton, Camburn, Alwin, & Young-DeMarco, 1988) to include retrospective questions to differentiate time frames. The questionnaire can be divided into two chronologically sequential timeframes. The first period includes items that ask about thoughts and behavior before the issue of protest emerged. The second period consists of items about thoughts and behavior after the issue of protest emerged but before the respondent went to the protest (for protestors) or during the time of the protest (for non-protestors). Thoughts and behavior may change after people protest, so it was necessary to track only thoughts and behavior that occurred before participation in the protest to identify potential factors that lead to protest. Using this survey design, it was possible to chronologically order factors and reduce the problem of endogeneity. For example, as protest-related social media activity is measured before the behavior of protest, the concern that people change their social media activity as a result of participating in the protest should be minimal.

This study selects a group who are biographically available by restricting the age range to 18–30. Eighteen is the average age at which students graduate from high school, and 30 is roughly when Taiwanese get married (Directorate General of Budget, Accounting and Statistics, 2014). However, a few respondents ($n = 37$) reported that their age was outside the range. Results do not change whether or not the cases are excluded from the analysis.

Sampling

The questionnaire was posted on a series of forums on PTT, a popular Bulletin Board System (BBS) that has been highly used by young people in Taiwan since 1983 (Shen, 1995). The number of users on PTT can exceed a hundred thousand simultaneously at its peak. Users use PPT as their primary daily routine for gaining information and socializing. PTT contains many forums that are categorized by topic (e.g., political issues, news, movies, etc.). In this study, respondents were mostly recruited from forums that have no connection to protest or politics. In other words, the questionnaire was purposely posted to avoid selecting on variables (e.g., political interest) that may be highly correlated with the dependent variable – protest activity. Controlling for possible board effects does not change the results. One should note that a representative random sample is not required, as this study is not aimed at estimating population proportions such as the percentage of the younger generation in Taiwan that participated in the Sunflower Movement. Instead, we are interested in the relationship between social media use and protest participation, which allows for valid estimation as we account for sources of selection bias (e.g., political interest, protest experience) in the models. As we are comparing levels of commitment between movement participants, non-participants (i.e., respondents who did not physically participate in the Sunflower Movement and had no activity on social media related to the movement) are removed from our analysis. The sample size for analysis is 801.

Measures

Three key concepts are of particular interest: physical participation in the protest, protest-related social media activity, and commitment. Physical participation was measured by a binary item: 'Did you physically participate in the Sunflower Movement?' (0 = no, 1 = yes). Protest-related social media activity was measured by a scale with five items (Cronbach's $\alpha = 0.9$):

> On your social media, how often did you (1) post comments on the Trade Agreement issue or the Sunflower Movement? (2) reply to other people's posts on the Trade Agreement issue or the Sunflower Movement? (3) repost or re-share other people's posts on the Trade Agreement issue or the Sunflower Movement? (4) 'like' other people's posts on the Trade Agreement issue or the Sunflower Movement and (5) encourage others to participate physically in the Sunflower Movement?

Respondents indicated their frequency on a five-point scale (1 = never, 5 = everyday). Note that by design if the respondent participated in the protest, this measures social media activity before he/she participated.

Measures of identification and efficacy follow previous work on psychological incentives in the collective action literature (see Opp, 2012; Opp & Kittel, 2009). Identification consists of two items ($\rho = 0.72$): 'In general, I felt close towards those who would physically attend the movement', 'In general, I admired those who would physically attend the movement' (1 = strongly disagree, 4 = strongly agree). Efficacy was measured by the item 'I felt that I would have an impact if I participated in the Sunflower Movement' (1 = strongly disagree, 4 = strongly agree).

We also asked for demographic variables including gender (0 = male, 1 = female), age, status as college student (0 = not student, 1 = college/graduate student) father's education and mother's education (1 = less than elementary school, 7 = doctoral), family income (0 = less than 30001 NTD, 5 = over 90001 NTD).

Several measures of previous political behavior were included as control variables, including 'On average, how often did you discuss political or social issues with others?' and 'On average, how often did you read political or social news?' (1 = less than once a month, 5 = everyday). Additional items measured whether the respondent ever had the experience of attending a protest, attending a political rally, attending a community meeting, working for a politician, working with an NGO, or solving community problems with others (0 = no, 1 = yes).

To illustrate our tests on H1 and H2, we use bar-plots and *t*-tests to assess differences between groups. For H3, we include control variables to describe the relationship between social media activity and offline protest participation. Descriptive statistics for the sample are provided below in Table 1.

Table 1. Descriptive statistics of measures.

	Descriptive statistics of measures		
Key variables	Range	Mean	SD
Protest	(0,1)	0.42	0.49
Social media activity	(6,25)	12.96	5.28
Identification	(2,8)	6.69	1.02
Efficacy	(1,4)	2.74	0.72
Control variables			
Discuss politics	(1,5)	2.65	1.21
Read political news	(1,5)	3.73	1.26
Protest experience	(0,5)	0.64	1.45
Internalized norms	(1,4)	2.69	0.72
Income	(1,6)	3.47	1.68

Results

Commitment levels of offline participants, online-only participants, and core social media participants

338 respondents in our sample participated offline at least once and 458 participated entirely online. We first compare levels of identification and efficacy between these online participants and physical participants. We found that offline participants have higher levels of both identification (p-value under t-test <.001) and sense of efficacy (p-value under t-test <.001). The result is supportive of our first hypothesis that offline participants are on average more committed than online-only participants.

However, our first test does not distinguish core social media participants from the online crowds. Therefore, the second test focuses on core social media participants (cloud activists), operationalized as online-only participants whose social media activity is one standard deviation higher than the mean.[1]

We find 49 core social media participants whose social media activity level is one standard deviation higher than the mean. That is more than 10% of all online-only participants. Compared to the previous result that physical participants have higher levels of commitment, t-test results suggest that the difference in efficacy levels between core social media participants and physical participants is not statistically significant ($p = .18$). Furthermore, results show that core social media participants have even higher levels of identification ($p < .05$) than offline participants. *H2* is supported in that core social media participants have a comparable level of commitment with offline participants.

To illustrate, Figure 1 compares identification and efficacy levels between online-only participants excluding core social media activists, offline participants, and core social media participants. Core social media participants have the highest levels of commitment comparable to offline participants and in general the online crowd has significantly lower levels (ANOVA analysis yield similar results). Thus, in contrast to the argument that online participants generally lack commitment, we find that those who are the most active on social media are also the most committed among all participants.

Relationship between social media activity and offline protest participation

Current studies predominantly utilize linear models to document a positive relationship between social media activity and offline mobilization (Castells, 2012; Harlow, 2012;

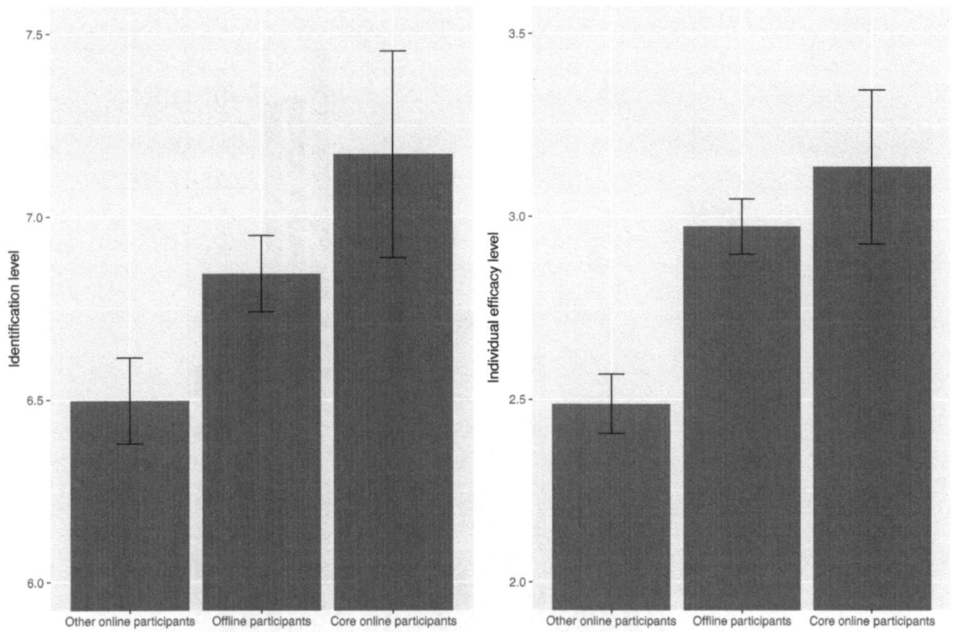

Figure 1. Identification and efficacy levels between other online participants, offline participants, and core online participant. Source: Authors' dataset.

Valenzuela, 2013). However, as the literature increasingly reveals, the online space may consist of different types of actors such as serial activists (Bastos & Mercea, 2016) or online spectators (Kavada, 2015). Different actors may have differential usage of social media, and thus implying *the relationship between social media and offline participation may not be linear.*

The bivariate relationship between protest-related social media activity and probability of offline participation is presented in Figure 2. On the horizontal axis is the level of social media activity, while the vertical axis represents the percentage that physically participated for each level. As seen, the relationship appears to be *curvilinear*. The mobilizing effect of social media activity on offline participation appears to be positive until a threshold (i.e., around the value of 19 or 20), and after the threshold we observe a dramatic decrease in the proportion that went to the Movement. For social media high-end users, their probability of offline participation is lower than those who have medium levels of social media activity.

The mobilizing effect of social media may be confounded by third variables such as political interest. Those who are more politically interested might be both more likely to be active on social media and participate in the protest. In order to account for potential confounding variables, we ran a Generalized Additive Model (GAM) (Hastie & Tibshirani, 1990) which allows non-parametric smoothing while also controlling for third variables. The advantage of a GAM is that it provides a flexible method to examine the functional form (i.e., identify non-linear relationships) between social media and protest while including control variables on socio-demographic variables, previous experiences of protest participation, discussing politics, reading political or social news to capture political interest before the trade agreement issue.

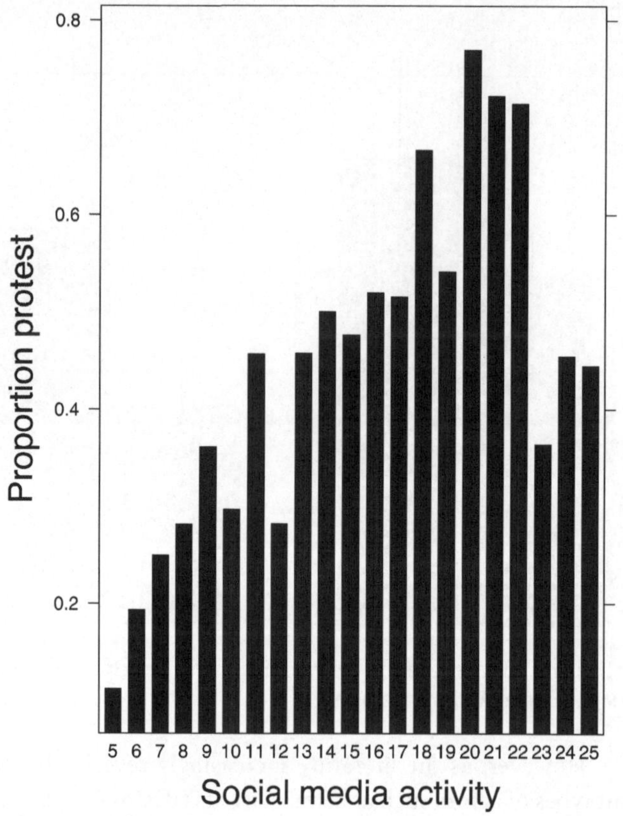

Figure 2. Bivariate relationship between level of social media activity and offline protest participation. Source: Authors' dataset.

In Figure 3, the horizontal axis represents social media activity and the vertical axis is a normalized index of probability of protest.[2] The curvilinear relationship in Figure 2 is observed. Social media activity has a positive effect on protest participation to a threshold. However, after the threshold there seems to be a negative relationship.

However, although GAMs allow us to inquire functional forms, they do not allow us to test whether the curvilinear relationship is statistically significant. Thus, we estimated a logistic regression model using offline protest participation as the outcome variable and social media activity as the explanatory variable with control variables that account for potential selection bias. Results are presented in Table 2.[3] The squared term for social media activity is statistically significant (which is equivalent to an *F*-test suggesting better model fit), and the direction of the term is negative, signifying an inverted U-shape relationship between social media activity and offline protest. Estimating alternative models with subsets of control variables does not change results. Furthermore, robustness checks suggest that the negative squared term is unlikely due to outliers (available upon request).

To illustrate, Figure 4 presents simulation results with *all control variables held at mean levels*, transferring into predicted probabilities since log-odds are difficult to interpret. Each simulation draws from the sampling distribution of the coefficients in the model, and transforms the predicted log-odds into the corresponding predicted-probabilities.[4] The horizontal axis is level of social media activity, while the vertical axis is the predicted

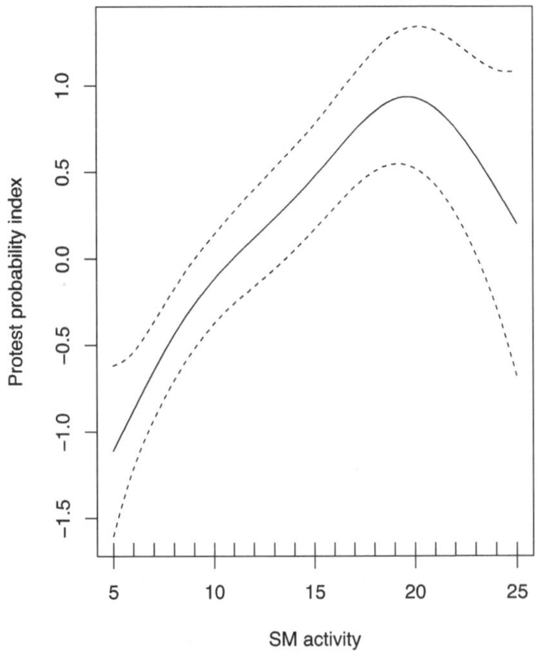

Figure 3. Generalized Additive Model smoothing between level of social media activity and offline protest participation. Source: Authors' dataset.

probability of physically participating in the Movement. Again we observe a curvilinear relationship between social media activity and offline protest probability, which is consistent with the GAM model above.

Thus, the results point to the curvilinear relationship between social media activity and offline protest probability. Before the threshold, social media usage related to

Table 2. Logistic regression estimates predicting protest participation.

Variables	Estimate	SE
Social media activity	0.36***	0.09
Social media activity (Squared)	−0.01**	0.00
Socio-demographic characteristics		
Female	0.32	0.20
Age	0.02	0.03
Father education	−0.13	0.13
Mother education	0.38**	0.13
Income	0.23***	0.06
Previous political experience		
Discuss politics	−0.03	0.09
Read political news	−0.17	0.09
Attended rally	0.28	0.27
Attended community meeting	0.45	0.27
Worked for politician	−0.15	0.57
Worked for NGO	0.34	0.34
Solved community problems	−0.84**	0.26
Attended protest	1.49***	0.28
Number of observations	609	
Nagelkerke Pseudo R^2	0.292	

Note. Standard errors in parentheses.
*$p < .05$, **$p < .01$, ***$p < .001$.

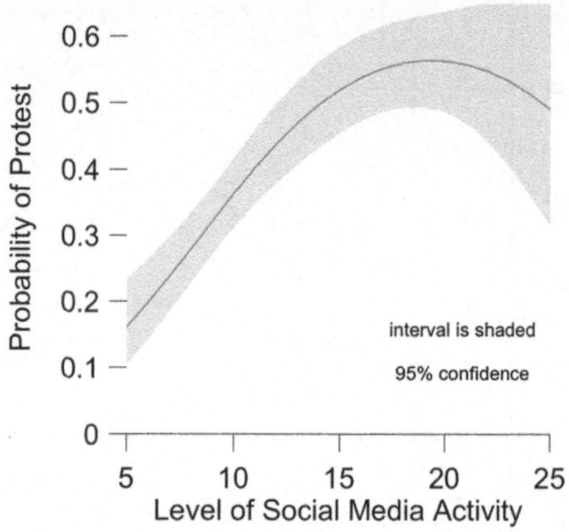

Figure 4. Visualization of relationship between social media activity and protest participation with all controls held at mean level. Source: Authors' dataset.

protest incentivizes people to physically participate in the movement. Beyond the threshold, high-level social media users are less likely to physically participate compare to their medium level counterparts. While current literature point to a positive effect of social media activity on offline participation (Castells, 2012; Harlow, 2012; Valenzuela, 2013), *H3* is rejected in light of a curvilinear relationship.

Preliminary analysis on characteristics of core online-only participants

Since we identify an interesting group of core online-only participants who are committed yet do not seem to participate online, one may be interested in the characteristics of such a unique group. Who are these core online-only participants, and how do they utilize tools of digital media? While such questions are beyond the scope of this study and require another systematically designed research, as a preliminary exploration we compare them with other participants in regard to their online activity and demographic characteristics. Note that these results are more descriptive than inferential, but they do provide insights on who the core online-only participants are.

First, we examine the specific social media activities of the core social media participants and compare with other participants. In Table 3, numbers in the first two columns are the average of the specific social media activity. Core online-only participants focus relatively more on responding to other online users' posts and encouraging other users to physically take part in the movement. This suggests that core social media participants may play a more significant role in intentionally engaging targeted audience for political discussion or mobilization.

Next, we examine demographic characteristics. Core online-only participants tend to be male and heavy consumers of political/social news, while differences in age, income, or street protest experience are not statistically significant. The fact that they consume relatively more news than others helps explain why they engage more in responding to other online users' posts and encouraging other users to physically take part in the movement, as both activities require political awareness.

Table 3. Comparison of social media activities.

Variable	Other participants	Core online participants	Difference
SM post	2.20	4.18	1.99
SM respond	2.32	4.55	2.23
SM repost/reshare	2.28	4.22	1.94
SM like	3.40	4.84	1.44
SM encourage participation	2.10	4.18	2.08
Number of observations	752	49	

Source: Authors' data.

Discussion and conclusion

Our study has two major findings. First, we found socio-psychological evidence for high commitment among a group of online-only social media participants. We demonstrated that their identification with the movement and sense of efficacy are at least on par with, if not necessarily higher than, the offline participants. This finding contradicts the traditional notion that only offline participation embodies high commitment and suggests that commitment can be actualized in online forms through sustained or highly intensive organizing activities. This finding of core social media participants who are amongst the most committed but opt not to physically participate fundamentally challenges the 'slacktivism' argument that writes off all social media participants as half-hearted identity shoppers. We call this group of core social media activists the 'cloud activists'. 'Cloud', as a metaphor, speaks to the dynamic and distributed nature of the protest space. It designates a virtual space where online networks and discourses constantly grow, interconnect, disjoin, or break down, which may or may not be connected with physical locations of contention. 'Activists', on the other hand, signifies invested and committed core participants, and sets them apart from bystander publics and half-hearted participants in the online crowd.

Our finding of 'cloud activists' is also validated by our finding of a non-linear relationship between social media activity and offline participation. The commonly held assumption of a linear relationship between offline participation and social media use suggests that heavy social media users tend to participate offline as social media use mobilizes people to take to the streets. However, we found a non-linear relationship between social media use and offline participation – social media only mobilizes offline participation among low and medium level social media users.

For highly active social media users, using social media is negatively associated with offline participation. In a general sense, we showed that the virtual space consists of different actor types, and such intricacies cannot be captured by linear models. Non-linear modeling, such as GAMs or other non-parametric explorations, is more helpful to tease out the complexity of political participation in the virtual space.

Thus, the results suggest that in the virtual space at least two types of digital production are in action. There is the peer-production process of connective action by online participants who are not necessarily psychologically committed to the collective cause, but may nonetheless contribute through collective efforts of the crowd (Bennett et al., 2014; Karpf, 2016). On the other hand, there are cloud activists who shoulder the responsibilities half-hearted participants cannot bear. In digitally enabled protests, commitment is not only embodied within the high-profile and high-risk offline activities such as march and hunger strikes, but also in the relatively behind-the-scene and mundane online work of linking and remixing, curating and sorting, preserving and archiving digital resources that also require personal sacrifice and persistent involvement. Committed cloud activists may play the role of what Taylor (1989) describes as 'abeyance structures' that enable movements to persist. Similar to the National Woman's Party in the Feminist Movement, these core social media activists may create conditions for other participants to coalesce around social media platforms that perform a variety of functions (Castells, 2012; Harlow, 2012; Valenzuela, 2013). Because of their consistent support, far from being ephemeral, digitally enabled protests should be able to possess characteristics of self-devotion and persistence required for success. Committed cloud activists may hold the key to understanding how digitally enabled protests persist, adapt, or transform over time.

Our findings about high commitment among social media participants also resonate with scholarly work on digital leadership. Recently, researchers in ICT and social movement studies started to focus on protest 'leadership' in reaction to claims of 'leaderlessness' and horizontality in recent digitally enabled large-scale protests. Gerbaudo (2016) used the term 'digital vanguards' to describe Facebook and Twitter admins in the Occupy movement; Poell et al., (2015) referred to Facebook admins in the 2011 Egyptian uprising as 'connective leaders' to highlight their marketing and branding strategies in administrating the Kullena Khaled Said Facebook page. The 'cloud activists' we found in the Sunflower movement that make more substantive contributions than typical clicktivists can also be seen as a type of 'virtual leaders' –people in the virtual space that consume more political news than others, constantly respond to other online users' posts, and encourage other users to physically take part in the movement with a high level of commitment to the cause. Thanks to social media, they may share the burden of street leaders, as they demonstrate the heart and will to undertake tasks designed for the committed, and possess the means to contribute via digital media.

The notion of cloud activist is transferrable to any digitally enabled protests. But the distribution of cloud activists in a particular movement should hinge upon the configuration of its protest networks and individual's understanding of his/her role in the movement. Protest networks with highly concentrated power signature (Bennett & Segerberg, 2013) may rely more on committed heavy contributors than ones with more dispersed structure. If committed activists find their time better spent online, we expect to see more cloud activists working judiciously to achieve their goals.

With a strong sense of identification and self-efficacy, these core social media activists in the Sunflower Movement found their talents and efforts best leveraged in the online space. Within a year, many participants of the Sunflower Movement coalesced into a new populist political party, the New Power Party, which became the third largest political party in the legislative body of Taiwan in 2016 (Chiu, 2016). These cloud activists may have played a crucial role in such a transition and adaption. Future studies should investigate their specific online activities, the composition of their online social network, and their relationship with the online crowd at large in co-producing the crowd-sourced organizational package, and their role in various protest phases such as mobilization, decline, and long-term adaption.

Notes

1. Changing the threshold to 1.5 SD does not change results.
2. The mean of the normalized index is set to zero.

3. The reduction of sample size is mainly because certain respondents were not sure about their commitment level, resulting in missing values.
4. See Adolph (2016). simcf: Counterfactuals and confidence intervals for estimated regression models. R package version 0.2.15.

Acknowledgements

We would like to thank the organizers and participants of the 'Digital Media, Political Polarization, and Challenges to Democracy' symposium for a great environment to discuss and improve our paper. We would also like to thank two anonymous reviewers for their useful comments. We are grateful for the thoughtful and constructive feedback on our earlier drafts from Prof. Steven Pfaff and Prof. Lance Bennett. Finally, we thank the Center for Studies in Demography and Ecology of the University of Washington for supporting the computing environment.

Disclosure statement

No potential conflict of interest was reported by the authors.

Notes on contributors

Yuan Hsiao is a Ph.D. candidate in Sociology and a Master's student in Statistics at the University of Washington. His areas of specialization are quantitative methods, social media, collective action, social networks, and social psychology. He has recently published in New Media & Society and the Routledge Taiwan Series on Taiwan's Social Movements.

Yunkang Yang is a Ph.D. Candidate in the Department of Communication at the University of Washington. His research areas include political communication, information and communication technology, and journalism. His dissertation is on disinformation and right wing media in the US. His research has been published on the International Journal of Communication, Asian Journal of Communication, and various Chinese academic journals.

ORCID

Yuan Hsiao http://orcid.org/0000-0002-8342-4938

References

Adolph, Christopher. (2016). simcf: Counterfactuals and confidence intervals for estimated regression models. R package version 0.2.17.

Bandura, A. (1982). Self-efficacy mechanism in human agency. *American Psychologist, 37*(2), 122.

Barbera, P., Wang, N., Bonneau, R., Jost, J., Nagler, J., Tucker, J., & Gonzalez-Bailon, S. (2015). The critical periphery in the growth of social protests. *PloS One, 10*(11), e0143611.

Bastos, M. T., & Mercea, D. (2016). Serial activists: Political Twitter beyond influentials and the twittertariat. *New Media & Society, 18*(10), 2359–2378.

Bennett, W. L. (1998). The uncivic culture: Communication, identity, and the rise of lifestyle politics. *PS: Political Science & Politics, 31*(04), 741–761.

Bennett, W. L. (2012). The personalization of politics: Political identity, social media, and changing patterns of participation. *The ANNALS of the American Academy of Political and Social Science, 644*(1), 20–39.

Bennett, W. L., & Segerberg, A. (2013). *The logic of connective action*. Cambridge, UK: Cambridge University Press.

Bennett, W. L., Segerberg, A., & Walker, S. (2014). Organization in the crowd: Peer production in large-scale networked protests. *Information, Communication & Society*, *17*(2), 232–260.

Berney, L. R., & Blane, D. (1997). Collecting retrospective data: Accuracy of recall after 50 years judged against historical records. *Social Science and Medicine*, *45*(10), 1519–1525.

Castells, M. (2012). *Networks of outrage and hope*. Cambridge: Polity Press.

Chen, H. T., Ping, S., & Chen, G. (2015). Far from reach but near at hand: The role of social media for cross-national mobilization. *Computers in Human Behavior*, *53*, 443–451.

Chiu, T. (2016, January). As the third largest party, New Power Party insists on reform. *United Daily News*.

Della Ratta, D., & Valeriani, A. (2014). Remixing the spring! Connective leadership and read-write practices in the 2011 Arab uprisings. In C. Padovani, & A. Calabrese (Eds.), *Communication Rights and Social Justice* (pp. 288–304). London: Palgrave Macmillan.

Directorate General of Budget, Accounting and Statistics. (2014). https://www.stat.gov.tw/ct.asp?xItem=15409&CtNode=3622&mp=4.

Finkel, S. E., Muller, E. N., & Opp, K. (1989). Personal influence, collective rationality, and mass political action. *The American Political Science Review*, *83*(3), 885.

Freedman, D., Thornton, A., Camburn, D., Alwin, D., & Young-DeMarco, L. (1988). The life history calendar: A technique for collecting retrospective data. *Sociological Methodology*, *18*(1), 37–68.

Freelon, D., McIlwain, C., & Clark, M. (2016). Quantifying the power and consequences of social media protest. *New Media and Society*, *20*(3), 990–1011.

Gamson, W. A. (1992). *Talking politics*. New York, NY: Cambridge University Press.

Gerbaudo, P. (2016). Social media teams as digital vanguards: The question of leadership in the management of key Facebook and Twitter accounts of Occupy Wall Street, Indignados and UK Uncut. *Information, Communication & Society*, *20*(2), 185–202.

Gil de Zúñiga, H., Jung, N., & Valenzuela, S. (2012). Social media use for news and individuals' social capital, civic engagement and political participation. *Journal of Computer-Mediated Communication*, *17*(3), 319–336.

Gladwell, M. (2010). Small change. *The New Yorker*, *4*(2010), 42–49.

González-Bailón, S., Borge-Holthoefer, J., & Moreno, Y. (2013). Broadcasters and hidden influentials in online protest diffusion. *American Behavioral Scientist*, *57*, 943–965.

Harlow, S. (2012). Social media and social movements: Facebook and an online Guatemalan justice movement that moved offline. *New Media & Society*, *14*(2), 225–243.

Hastie, T. J., & Tibshirani, R. J. (1990). *Generalized additive models*. London: Chapman & Hall.

Ho, M. S. (2015). Occupy Congress in Taiwan: Political opportunity, threat, and the Sunflower Movement. *Journal of East Asian Studies*, *15*(1), 69–97.

Jurgenson, N. (2012). When atoms meet bits: Social media, the mobile web and augmented revolution. *Future Internet*, *4*(1), 83–91.

Karpf, D. (2014). Comment on 'Organization in the crowd: Peer production in large-scale networked protests'. *Information, Communication & Society*, *17*(2), 261–263.

Karpf, D. (2016). *Analytic activism: Digital listening and the new political strategy*. Oxford: Oxford University Press.

Kavada, A. (2015). Creating the collective: Social media, the Occupy Movement and its constitution as a collective actor. *Information, Communication & Society*, *18*(8), 872–886.

Klandermans, B. (2002). How group identification helps to overcome the dilemma of collective action. *American Behavioral Scientist*, *45*(5), 887–900.

Klandermans, B., & de Weerd, M. (2000). Group identification and political protest. In S. Stryker, T. J. Owens, & R. W. White (Eds.), *Self, identity, and social movements* (pp. 68–90). Minneapolis, MN: University of Minnesota Press.

Margetts, H., John, P., & Yasseri, T. (2015). *Political turbulence*. Princeton, NJ: Princeton University Press.

McAdam, D. (1986). Recruitment to high-risk activism: The case of freedom summer. *American Journal of Sociology*, *92*(1), 64–90.

Morell, M. F. (2012). The free culture and 15M movements in Spain: Composition, social networks and synergies. *Social Movement Studies, 11*(3–4), 386–392.
Morgan, G. S., & Chan, W. Y. (2016). Different paths to protest: Predictors of collective action in the occupy movement. *Journal of Applied Social Psychology, 46*(10), 565–582. doi:10.1111/jasp.12386
Morozov, E. (2011). *The net delusion: The dark side of internet freedom*. New York, NY: Public Affairs.
Opp, K. (2012). Collective identity, rationality and collective political action. *Rationality and Society, 24*(1), 73–105.
Opp, K., & Kittel, B. (2009). The dynamics of political protest: Feedback effects and interdependence in the explanation of protest participation. *European Sociological Review, 26*(1), 97–109.
Penney, J., & Dadas, C. (2014). (Re) Tweeting in the service of protest: Digital composition and circulation in the Occupy Wall Street movement. *New Media & Society, 16*(1), 74–90.
Pfaff, S., Hechter, M., & Corcoran, K. E. (2016). The problem of solidarity in insurgent collective action: The Nore mutiny of 1797. *Social Science History, 40*(02), 247–270.
Poell, T., Abdulla, R., Rieder, B., Woltering, R., & Zack, L. (2015). Protest leadership in the age of social media. *Information, Communication & Society, 19*(7), 994–1014.
Porter, L. W., Crampon, W. J., & Smith, F. J. (1976). Organizational commitment and managerial turnover: A longitudinal study. *Organizational Behavior and Human Performance, 15*(1), 87–98.
Robertson, P. J., & Tang, S.-Y. (1995). The role of commitment in collective action: Comparing the organizational behavior and rational choice perspectives. *Public Administration Review, 55*(1), 67.
Rowen, I. (2015). Inside Taiwan's Sunflower Movement: Twenty-four days in a student-occupied parliament, and the future of the region. *The Journal of Asian Studies, 74*(1), 5–21.
Saunders, C., Grasso, M., Olcese, C., Rainsford, E., & Rootes, C. (2012). Explaining differential protest participation: Novices, returners, repeaters, and stalwarts. *Mobilization: An International Quarterly, 17*(3), 263–280.
Shen, W.C. (1995). *The Applications of Internet Skills of Internet/Fidonet*. Taipei: Songgang.
Specht, D., & Ros-Tonen, M. A. (2016). Gold, power, protest: Digital and social media and protests against large-scale mining projects in Colombia. *New Media & Society, 19*(12), 1907–1926.
Taiwan Network Information Center. (2014). Retrieved from http://www.twnic.net.tw/download/200307/20140820c.pdf
Tajfel, H., & Turner, J. C. (1979). An integrative theory of intergroup conflict. *The Social Psychology of Intergroup Relations, 33*(47), 74.
Taylor, V. (1989). Social movement continuity: The women's movement in abeyance. *American Sociological Review, 54*(5), 761–775.
Tilly, C. (2004). *Social movements, 1768–2004*. Boulder, CO: Paradigm.
Tufekci, Z., & Wilson, C. (2012). Social media and the decision to participate in political protest: Observations from Tahrir Square. *Journal of Communication, 62*(2), 363–379.
Valenzuela, S. (2013). Unpacking the use of social media for protest behavior: The roles of information, opinion expression, and activism. *American Behavioral Scientist, 57*(7), 920–942.
van Zomeren, M., Postmes, T., & Spears, R. (2008). Toward an integrative social identity model of collective action: A quantitative research synthesis of three socio-psychological perspectives. *Psychological Bulletin, 134*(4), 504–535.
Xing, Q., & Jin, J. (2014). The role of new media in Taiwan's Sunflower Movement. *Taiwan Research Journal [in Chinese], 136*(6), 16–24.
Zhou, Y. Q., & Yang, Y. K. (2017). Media strategy of social contentions in China: Comparing environmental and land requisition protests. *Communication & Society, 40*, 169–202. [in Chinese].

6 Counter-surveillance and alternative new media in Turkey

Bora Ataman and Barış Çoban

ABSTRACT

This study, drawing on alternative media and networked social movements, explores the counter-surveillance practices and oppositional imaginaries of activist citizen journalists (ACJs) in Turkey to combat the surveillance strategies of the authoritarian Turkish government. After the failed coup attempt in July 2016, the ruling party has become more suspicious of dissent of any kind. However, the ACJs who use mobile communication and social media as channels for journalism and counter-surveillance continue their critical journalistic work in this context. Using ethnographic data collected from interviews with these media activists, this study focuses on oppositional imaginaries regarding the surveillance culture as well as counter-surveillance tactics, both offensive and defensive. To do so, we conducted 22 in-depth interviews with the representatives of alternative new media (ANM) initiatives and ACJs who were gathering, producing and disseminating news at the time of the study (between January and July 2017). Backed by the available literature on interdisciplinary approaches, data were gathered from the interviews, thematically coded and critically analysed. The whole process of news-making that criticises the authoritarian surveillance state stands out as an offensive tactic. On the other hand, defensive tactics are very closely related to the safety of journalists, their sources and data. The paper argues that the variety of offensive and defensive tactics should be increased and they should be substantially improved. The study also sheds light on the need for more detailed and extensive interdisciplinary research.

Introduction

Neoliberal globalization is destroying the relationship between modern states and democracy. Any concept of the citizen that refers to democratic rights pleases neither authoritarian right-wing populist leaders nor their corporate backers. Once these leaders are in power, they resent being accountable to the electorate, and believe in their right to install mass surveillance mechanisms within the country and even abroad, as Snowden's leaks make clear. In short, as Bennett (2017) warns, the liberal democratic paradigm giving citizens the political right, among others, to hold governments accountable is gradually regressing into paternalistic and authoritarian patterns in many countries, including

Turkey (Topak, 2017; Yeşil & Sözeri, 2017). Recent reports and indexes support these claims (Freedom House, 2017a; The EIU, 2017; WJP, 2018).

Nonetheless, the struggles of networked social movements (NSMs)for better democracy (Castells, 2012; Juris, 2004) are spreading globally. Contemporary pro-democratic and multi-issue social movements (SMs) such as the *anti-globalization*, *Indignados*, and *Occupy* movements, which have spread across the world in recent years, support this argument with factual evidence (Bennett & Segerberg, 2013; Castells, 2012; Gerbaudo, 2012; Harcourt, 2013; Harvey, 2014; Tükekçi, 2017; Zizek, 2012). A local Turkish example with global ties is the Gezi Resistance movement of June 2013 (Tuğal, 2013). Furthermore, the role of information and communication technologies in these struggles is vital; they channel what Castells describes as '... movements spread by contagion in a world networked by the wireless Internet' (2012, p. 2), even though the movements' dependence on digital infrastructure also strengthens the repressive surveillance strategies of the state against them (e.g., Boykoff, 2006; Davenport, Johnston, & Mueller, 2005; Liestert, 2012).

By drawing upon theories of alternative new media (ANM), counter-surveillance and NSMs, the present study argues that the counter-surveillance tactics of the ANM – of news platforms and activist citizen journalists (ACJs) – should be considered essential if democratic ideals are to be kept alive and improved by bottom-up constituents of democracy such as deliberative and direct participation (Held, 1987). We argue that resisting authoritarian repression; preserving the solidarity between dissident circles in fragmented societies; informing the public about inappropriate schemes from the ruling elite; and ultimately revitalizing the mechanisms of democratic decision-making are all needed in today's democracies, including Turkey. Therefore, the need becomes self-evident to produce news and analyses that contribute to the critical distance from politics that every citizen needs.

Thus, the aim of this study is first to understand the oppositional imaginaries and relevant counter-surveillance practices of the suppliers of alternative news who resist the surveillance strategies of the present Turkish government. The latter seeks to curb every journalistic practice deemed detrimental to the 'national interest' and its own authority. Ethnographic data gathered through semi-structured in-depth interviews helped us to pursue our goal. Second, by critically compiling and analysing the state's surveillance tactics we hope to contribute to the news activists' repertoire with something more operational and useful. We want this interdisciplinary research to link the fields of ANM and counter-surveillance, opening the way for other research.

Theoretical framework

Convergence yet to come

With regard to scholarly work, NSMs have a positive impact on reducing the gaps and even creating overlaps between alternative media (AM), social movements, and surveillance studies. The research that skilfully connects SMs and the AM (Atkinson, 2010; Dencik & Wilkin, 2015; Downing, Ford, Gil, & Stein, 2001; Gerbaudo, 2012; Lievrouw, 2011) has significantly expanded. Furthermore, the recent special edition of *Digital Journalism* focuses on the interaction between a surveillance society and journalism (Wahl-Jorgensen,

Hintz, Dencik, & Bennett, 2017). While surveillance studies more frequently tackle the concept of resistance (e.g., Fernandez & Huey, 2009; Hermida & Hernández-Santaolalla, 2017; Mann, Nolan, & Wellman, 2003; Marx, 2016), however, its relevance to the fields of AM and ASM mentioned above is still obscure.

By slightly expanding upon Lievrouw's (2011) theorization, we argue that the important role of standing up to authoritarian rule and ubiquitous mass surveillance could fall to 'alternative and activist new media', which consist of networks of activist digital citizens who can also be viewed as volunteer new media workers, communication agents, and journalists of the networked movements. Dialogue and solidarity action distributed through networks of interconnected media activists are among the most effective ways of counter-surveillance, circumventing the hostile attempts by authoritarian states to constrain journalistic practices (Lievrouw, 2011, pp. 149–176; Nayar, 2015, pp. 158–174). This is because gathering, producing and disseminating information and news stories of public interest are much easier within distributed solidarity networks (Castells, 2012). New media, as Lievrouw states, 'provide the necessary platforms for participatory journalism' and participatory democracy (Lievrouw, 2011, p. 14). Similarly, alternative and activist media accounts in Turkey have higher levels of sharing and collaborative practice, which are more effective than those of the pro-government mainstream media (Doğu, 2017, pp. 7–9, 11).

'Citizenless democracy'

Writers such as Bennett (2017), Harcourt (2013), Harvey (2014), McChesney and Nichols (2016) and Zizek (2012) note that the hegemony of the global neoliberal market is circumventing democracy. Therefore, 'citizenless democracy' (McChesney & Nichols, 2016) has been usefully coined to describe countries within which political decisions are passed behind closed doors, houses of parliament stagnate, and nation-state rule rests with transnational market powers free of any kind of external supervision. Bennett (2017) focuses on the rise of right-wing political parties at a time when the citizens favouring liberal democracy have retreated from the stage of political elections, and on the way in which authoritarian leaders – the practitioners of the neoliberal agenda – polarize the public, consolidate their power by populist propaganda, and damage the democratic political system.

The struggle for democracy, admittedly a damaged ideal, continues. Scholars such as Harvey and Harcourt highlight the transformative power of SMs such as *Occupy* and *Gezi*. Harcourt observes that, replacing the mythical liberal democracy, versatile and multi-dimensional experiments in radical democracy based on deliberation, participation, and direct democracy are emerging worldwide through acts of civil/political disobedience (2013, p. 63). Yet these endeavours are suppressed by violent action at the hands of the police state. In fact, according to Hobsbawm (2007, pp. 132, 136–137), as the world-wide hegemony of neoliberal globalization is creating more SMs to disturb the dominant system, the political violence which has become systematically global creates a 'climate of fear' in the world. The result is a continuous sense of threat, a ubiquitous mass surveillance-supported global security mechanism and totalitarian democracy (Andrejevic, 2017; Harvey, 2014; Murakami Wood, 2017; Wahl-Jorgensen et al., 2017).

Surveillance culture

Living in a surveillance-supported weakened democracy or losing digital freedom and privacy provokes a little reaction from citizens, according to Dencik and Cable (2017). Following Bauman et al. (2014), we argue that this may be based on at least two factors, namely *familiarity* and *fear*. Familiarity is related to concepts such as 'surveillance realism' (Dencik & Cable, 2017) or postpanoptic 'environmental surveillance' (Andrejevic, 2017), where all the surveillance-related techniques become an ordinary and widespread part of daily life. Fear of the unpredictable dangers of modern life and a desire for security make citizens obedient. Citizens may even become fearful informants who actively participate in 'lateral surveillance' (Nayar, 2015), strengthening the police state (Ganascia, 2010).

Therefore, according to Lyon (2017, p. 826), popular concepts such as 'Big Brother' (Orwell, 1949) and 'Panopticon' (Foucault, 1977) or the 'Surveillance Society' and 'Surveillance State' (Lyon, 1994, 2001) are no longer adequate to convey 'contemporary late-modern conditions or, simply, digital modernity'. These concepts are mostly related to society's understanding of self-discipline and self-control without the power to connect or communicate with peers under the unilateral gaze of a higher power which can punish. Instead, Lyon proposes the concept of a 'surveillance culture', which involves active participation in surveillance. Obviously, while some willingly become an obedient part of this culture, others oppose and resist it (2017, pp. 824–825).

The surveillance imaginaries and practices of the activist citizens show that they are active participants courageous enough to follow collective dreams of creating a better, a civic, and a more humane life. However, the resistance of activist citizens to the controlling behaviour and hardware and software of surveillance (e.g., Zuboff, 2016, p. 2) is limited to developing whatever temporary tactics they can (e.g., Andrejevic, 2017; Leistert, 2012). Marx likens this to a cat and mouse game, whereby both sides as they learn to play adapt their offensive and defensive behaviours; or to a fiery social dance between opposing powers through strategic moves, counter-moves, and counter-counter moves (2016, p. 168).

Resistance …

ANM are valuable components as the nodes, or hubs, of 'networked' (Juris, 2004) or 'internetworked' (Langman, 2005) social movements, where much of the coordination and collaboration between media activists takes place, useful information is disseminated and news is transmitted (Atton, 2002; Downing et al., 2001; Juris, 2005; Lievrouw, 2011). Furthermore, the networks established in cyber-space tend to expand to fit urban space (Castells, 2012). These long- or short-term 'collective actions' mobilized for/against societal changes (Bennett & Segerberg, 2013) are mostly realized through solidarity networks where information and communication technologies play a crucial role in changing/transforming the organizational and communicational structures of social movements (Castells, 2012; Lievrouw, 2011).

Thus, we cannot understand contemporary multi-issue social movements without the heterarchical network structure (Van Dijk, 2012) empowered by the Internet in general and the socially enhanced Web 2.0 in particular; we must trace how it encourages autonomous individuals to communicate and collaborate, then act accordingly (Gerbaudo,

2012; Tuğal, 2013; Tükekçi, 2017). This argument suggests that 'citizen journalists' (Allan, 2009; Radsch, 2011; Rosen, 2006) or, from an activist perspective, 'activist citizen journalists' (Ataman & Çoban, 2017) are indeed constituent parts of a dissident and networked mediascape. They are amongst the journalists who serve to re-integrate fragmented multi-issue movements by linking activists from different spheres of society to movements and help to create common forums for participatory debate.

Their way of doing journalism echoes Deuze's 'participatory journalism' (Deuze, 2005) or 'alternative journalism' (Atton & Hamilton, 2008) in which collaboration is a way of gathering, writing, and disseminating news as well as forming communities around news-making. In fact, as implied by Doğu's research on Turkey's news media landscape through a network analysis of Twittersphere, 'the nonmainstream media – representing the civic network of dissident voices – bring together different segments of society around common issues and provide multifold aspects in the coverage of these issues' (Doğu, 2017, p. 16).

The alternative/activist new media, based on the collaboration of 'digital activist citizens' (Hintz, Dencik, & Wahl-Jorgensen, 2017; Isın & Ruppert, 2015), are in the communicational/informational vanguard. While the communicational front empowers horizontal movements and solidarity, the informational front provides needful instant information and, at the same time, creates a collective memory for the movement. However, the relative successes of all these are directly proportional to being protected, mainly from the eyes of the state. Offensive actions taken without defensive measures are highly risky. And in Turkey's government-controlled mainstream mediascape it is evidently an offence to use alternative and/or participatory methods in journalism (Doğu, 2017). The spectrum of risk is wide: from being manhandled and threatened with imprisonment to actual imprisonment and even death.

Understanding Turkey

Journalism in so-called liberal democratic states, according to Carlsson and Pöyhtäri (2017, p. 12), has increasingly become dysfunctional due to 'new forms of censorship and repression, self-censorship, surveillance, monitoring and control, gatekeeping, propaganda/disinformation, acts of terror, anti-terror laws, the criminalization of encryption and/or anonymity, hate speech and harassment, and organized crime.' This dysfunctioning is obvious in semi-democratic states such as Malaysia, Singapore, Russia, and Venezuela (Hem, 2014). Turkey, in the front line of such practices, has recently turned into a dangerous country, where the rule of law, civil liberties, and democratic governance are in sharp decline (The EIU, 2017; WJP, 2018).

The ruling Justice and Development Party (AKP), since it came to power in 2002, has not refrained from stifling the media, nor from declaring in harmony with neoliberal market capitalism its authoritarian stance on law-enforcement (Kurban & Sözeri, 2012; Topak, 2017; Yeşil & Sözeri, 2017). However, the violently suppressive policies against political uprisings and rebellious movements since the Gezi Resistance have intensified with every new dissident act (Freedom House, 2013; HRW, 2016). The political and legal actions taken to switch from a parliamentary to a presidential government system, in particular, alongside the State of Emergency declared after the failed coup of 15 July 2016, have kick-started discussions about changing from authoritarian democracy to single-party dictatorship (Topak, 2017, p. 541). As confirmed by many international chronicles, reports, and indexes, Turkey has now become more and more barren to democracy in general and journalism in particular (see Article 19; CPJ; Freedom House, 2017a, 2017b; The EIU, 2017; WJP, 2018). On the RSF Press Freedom Index (2017), Turkey is ranked 155 of 180 countries, below Russia (148) and Venezuela (151).

According to figures reported in January 2017, almost 70,000 social media accounts have been under surveillance since July 2016 (Freedom House/FOTN, 2017). Approximately 4000 people, of whom 1700 were arrested, were taken into custody due to their social media postings (Topak, 2017, p. 536; Yeşil & Sözeri, 2017, pp. 544, 546). In the last few years, more than 100 media outlets have been closed and 151 journalists and media workers have been jailed, according to the Journalists' Union of Turkey (TGS, 26 January 2018), while over 1000 journalists are unemployed.

The remaining alternative voices have been weakened by the widespread assault on critical journalism, the shrinking of dissident networks and the climate of fear under the surveillance state, according to the many international reports mentioned above. Some of the arrests were in response to leaks from hacked reports written by government authorities; the imprisoned writers are charged with terrorist propaganda, having published news about issues of public interest discussed in these documents (Diken, 2017).

In this context well-known celebrity journalists working for mainstream media had to become activists and now can make themselves heard only in the AM: for example, Nevşin Mengü, Ayşenur Arslan, and İrfan Değirmenci are now working as columnists for the leftist daily *Birgün*. Others who have established their own ANM platforms include the prominent author and former editor-in-chief of the daily *Cumhuriyet* Can Dündar, with *#özgürüz* (https://ozguruz.org and the experienced journalist Ruşen Çakır, with *Medya-Scope* (medyascope.tv). So, contradicting Hem's assertions (2014, pp. 5–6), it is not the conventional journalists working for the mainstream but the members of Turkey's alternative and activist new media who are seeking 'ways to circumvent censors' and 'exploit the cracks in the system' or ignore openly directed threats.

Despite the hostility, ANM (i.e., news platforms and ACJs) have emerged as oases of journalism. They act with the desire to empower people and to defend such fundamental democratic rights as *freedom of expression* and the *right to information*. Thus, they are presumed to protect their sources and their data, as well as themselves. Developing applicable and rewarding tactics against ubiquitous mass surveillance should in this context be considered a lifesaving activity.

Method

The method of this study is ethnographic data collection and qualitative analysis, in line with our theoretical approach, which is basically an AM theory from the standpoint of critical cultural studies or 'meaning-making' (Baran & Davis, 2012, pp. 247–280; Brennen, 2013, p. 9). However, our aim is not only ethnography's typical aim to capture people's sociocultural subjective moods, feelings and behaviours, but also to produce 'critical understandings that can help activists develop strategies to overcome obstacles and barriers to effective organizing' (Juris & Khasnabish, 2013, p. 4) with respect to counter-surveillance tactics. Therefore, we examine dissident experiences in the 'surveillance culture' throughout the AM sphere (Lyon, 2017; Marx, 2016).

The in-depth interviews were adapted according to questions and findings of prior studies of surveillance, AM, and social movements. The interviews focused on ACJs' tactics, both offensive and defensive, and all were sound-recorded, transcribed, and coded thematically. However, the names of the participants were never added to the transcripts and after completing each transcription we deleted the recording, mindful of the current political and legal risks. The transcripts were used in subsequent analyses. No digital footprints have been left.

The core questions of the interview guide are as follows: 'Can you identify the main safety/security risks (both real and virtual) in gathering, writing and disseminating news?'; 'How do you tackle offline and online surveillance of the state while working?'; 'Do you have pre-arranged procedures for the safety of news sources and subjects?'; 'Do you have ways to obstruct or confuse state surveillance?'; Do you think that sousveillance is an effective response to state surveillance?' We also referred to current affairs in guiding the interviewees, to encourage them to critically reflect on their own 'beliefs, attitudes, values and motivations' (Gaskell, 2000, p. 39) underlying their behaviours under surveillance.

Between January and July 2017, we held 22 in-depth, semi-structured interviews, in İstanbul, 12 with the representatives of ANM initiatives and 10 with ACJs. All our respondents were young adult graduates (aged 24–35). Each interview took approximately 2 hours. These relatively small numbers represent almost one-third of the active ANM and ACJs concerned. In the Gezi Resistance period, the numbers were markedly higher. The decline, specifically after the 'state of emergency', makes it easier to follow these activists. But the problems of safety they now face prevent the names of the initiatives and of the interviewees from disclosure. Moreover, to protect their identities, we avoided direct quotations as far as possible and tried to obscure links between speakers' identities and the content.

In exploring the tactics of activists (Marx, 2016) against the sanctioned surveillance system in Turkey, we use 'counter-surveillance' as an umbrella term for anything that opposes any of the state's strategies and tactics. State systems combine mass and targeted surveillance and are backed by pro-government professional and/or volunteer informants who range from the bureaucracy to academy, and from the private sector to civil society, whether offline or online (Topak, 2017; Yeşil & Sözeri, 2017). Yet our ethnographic approach and interview data gives us a cognitive understanding of Turkey's surveillance-related practices from the interviewees' perspective and provides the opportunity to assess counter-surveillance imaginaries and tactics critically.

Analysis and discussion

Offensive tactics

First, alternative and activist news-making gives clear evidence of offensive tactics in these compelling circumstances. In fact, when Marx discussed 12 neutralization techniques, he gave examples that can be evaluated in terms of video activism and citizen journalism (pp. 166–167) using his phrase 'taking advantage of the double edge potential of tools' (2016, p. 145).

Other works use the same concept in similar contexts (de Souza, 2014; Hermida & Hernández-Santaolalla, 2017; Wilson, 2012; Wilson & Serisier, 2010). However, the meaning of Monahan's dictum, 'counter-surveillance is defined as intentional, tactical uses, or disruption of surveillance technologies to challenge institutional power asymmetries' (Monahan, 2006, p. 515), expands the offensive force of the concept by considering its disruptive aspects.

Together with video activism, hacking and leaking journalism, which Nayar (2015, pp. 158–169) classifies under 'dissident surveillance', may be evaluated as disruptive journalistic practices of this kind. Ataman and Çoban (2016) also define counter-surveillance activities - citizen journalism and video activism, leaking, and hacking - as the three related fields of the informational struggle against authoritarian rule.

Therefore, in terms of news production, we argue that there are relatively new offensive techniques that exceed the limits drawn by traditional codes of journalism. Obviously they are not in the remit of the mainstream media in Turkey, which have already lost much to the cause of government and have little left with which to be independent, critical, or investigative in any sense. In this hostile environment acts of so-called counter-surveillance are vital and can be performed only by courageous ACJs and AMs. Some journalistic counter-surveillance techniques, it is thought, have been to make the targeted institutions transparent, to ridicule them and render them dysfunctional (Lievrouw, 2011; Nayar, 2015). After all, each journalistic act and its content are part of a societal power struggle, especially in countries such as Turkey where the rule of law, as the above reports and indexes indicate, is gradually weakening.

News production, the basic counter-surveillance practice of ACJs, is also the practice of explicit and/or implicit revelation of the violence of the state. The alternative outlets have served as the eye of the public, as they have in many other parts of the world (de Souza, 2014; Nayar, 2015; Rice, 2017; Shaw, 2013; Waghorn, 2016) In our interviews, ACJs, as 'digital activist citizens' (Isın & Ruppert, 2015), stated that in many cases they revealed the explicit or implicit violence of the state forces directed against outspoken individuals. Recording such violence through counter-surveillance becomes an important part of the legal and social struggle to uncover the assaults committed, as one of our respondents remarks:

> We recorded the disproportionate violence and the crimes committed by the police during the Gezi Resistance. Once, my recordings were used for the case of an activist, who was blinded by a gas cartridge shot by the police.

In addition to exposing the 'disproportionate' violence of the security forces through images taken by ACJs, their documenting of many cases that resulted in injury and death proves that ACJs have a crucial function in exposing the guilty. ACJs note that they have often made it possible to detect an officer who has committed an offence while operating in a dissident neighbourhood. Yet the culture of impunity devalues the work of activist journalists in today's Turkey.

The police strive to develop new methods in order to prevent journalists from obtaining any images or footage. In a case in Ankara in October 2017, the police encircled a group of demonstrators with their riot shields and prevented journalists from taking images of demonstrators as they were being beaten. One ACJ whom we interviewed, unlike the professionals at the scene, apparently found a way to circumvent this tactic:

> An NGO [official] was standing in a spot which overlooked the scene of the protest. I rushed there and took some shots. Then I sent these to the CJ collective where I volunteer. These

> images were disseminated in the social media … almost all alternative media institutions shared these images immediately …

Another ACJ with a fake identity card sneaked into a secret court where a case was being tried, pretending to be a professional journalist. Journalists were not allowed to take any photos whatsoever. Despite the danger, s/he also managed to take a photo unobserved which s/he posted on Twitter. In the photo, one of the judges in a highly sensitive case of a young man being shot and killed by the police during the Gezi Resistance seemed to be asleep. The photo immediately made its way onto the social media as well as headlines in the press, both ANM and mainstream (BİA, 2014). Not surprisingly, this journalistic act led to a police investigation against the journalist. However, our correspondent stated that s/he changed the name of the account immediately afterwards and still at the time of the interview had not been traced. These tactical actions are called 'avoiding and switching moves' and have their place among Marx's 'neutralization moves' (2016, p. 143).

Surveillance is also newsworthy for ACJs because they turn the issue of surveillance into news and open it up to public debate. In terms of creating awareness of surveillance and justifying counter-surveillance or sousveillance actions (Mann et al., 2003; Monahan, 2015), acts against the CCTV cameras set up to spy on neighbourhood social protests become news when ACJs record militants finding different ways to dislodge them. In addition, the police use drones to try to reach the areas that cannot be viewed by CCTV (Waghorn, 2016). However, militants have various ways of attacking the drones, sometimes by means of fireworks or firearms. In their news, the ACJs show militant counter-surveillance acts as part of a social struggle. According to one of our correspondents, showing that the state is not indestructible stiffens people's morale.

Despite these offensive practices, ACJs are cautious about the part that online hacking and leaking government sources should play in their journalism. We observed during our interviews with the news collectives that they keep their distance from online hacking. They made it clear that they pass on information that does not conflict with their own political and ethical approach and that, in their opinion, is for the common good. They are not in contact with hacker groups and have no intention of following their example:

> While it was an easy task, we did not contact *Redhack* or *Anonymous*. We prefer to make news out of the documents they reveal. Obviously, if it fits our ethical approach …

With regard to activating leaked journalism in Turkey, which is in fact similar to Greenwald's *The Intercept* (Rice, 2017), Turkey had a *Pirate Party Turkey* project called *Kara Kutu (Black Box)* in 2015 (Özel & Uyanık, 2016). It was planned to be an enabler for whistleblowers to leak news in full confidentiality and anonymity, but the plan was shelved due to the country's worsening political atmosphere. Nevertheless, members of an ANM collective whom we interviewed mentioned that they had openly supported the *Kara Kutu* project from its earliest days and they wanted to be involved in similar efforts in the near future.

> It would be completely insane to do it right now! Our lawyers noted that according to the anti-terror laws that have recently been passed such actions can be deemed acting as an enemy spy or being a part of a terrorist organization and can incur long-term imprisonment, whatever … We're insane anyway!

In the digital security training sessions offered by ANM to their volunteer activist journalists, the same recent legal developments are recalled and trainees are warned not to be part of illegally offensive practices of this kind. This implies that the training mostly concerns how to be safe under surveillance.

Defensive tactics

Defensive practices usually relate to the safety of the news and the activist journalists. Journalists are subjects of surveillance almost everywhere (Mills & Sarikakis, 2016; Wahl-Jorgensen et al., 2017). Therefore, they should be able to protect themselves from the eyes of the state in ways that include digital security (Carlsson & Pöyhtäri, 2017). Digital footprints and location-based surveillance could harm journalists (Sambrook, 2016, pp. 29–33). It has become habitual for law enforcers in countries such as Turkey to threaten journalists, damage their gear and tools, and seize and destroy any data they collect.

In Turkey journalists' homes, offices, and newspapers are raided and their electronic devices and documents are seized, to the point where such actions have become ordinary, as stated in many of the reports referred to above. But anyone who keeps track every week of what is happening to journalism can follow the 'Turkey Crackdown Chronicle' by the 'Committee to Protect Journalists' (CPJ) (https://cpj.org). In this situation, developing effective defence tactics is vital for news production and the protection of media resources, news subjects, journalists, and their organizations. The tactics should include offline and online platforms simultaneously. In periods of a 'state of exception' in Turkey, there is no legal basis for defending the crucial right of communication confidentiality accorded elsewhere to journalism. Sadly, Turkey is not alone in this regard (e.g., Mills and Sarikakis, 2016, pp. 9–10).

Therefore, in addition to the offline tactics developed for avoiding surveillance (including determining and deactivating possible surveillance tools and equipment all around them, knowing and avoiding regions with high surveillance, taking advantage of times, locations, and weather conditions that will render surveillance inefficient, wearing unobtrusive clothes, acting in the same manner and if necessary, changing physical appearance, not carrying sensitive documents without protection, blending in with the crowds and acting like part of the setting, preferring public transport, not being alone except when necessary, and going on news hunts with other activist journalists in the same trust group, etc.), online tactics such as using specially protected hardware, and encrypted software and applications should be used in coordination (Henrichsen, Betz, & Lisosky, 2015; Leistert, 2012; Marx, 2016; Monahan, 2006).

Self-defence is primary in the defensive practices of ACJs. In other words, in order to avoid the eyes of the government, it is crucial to determine which surveillance tactics to deploy and how to use them to take the necessary measures.

Offline and online (digital) security, then, is intricate, and cannot be split up for review. ACJs need to reach the field in order to carry out their activities under the surveillance of the state, and have to be careful during news production in the face of police inspection and/or attack. As the interview data show, ACJs disguise themselves in order to be allowed into demonstration areas without being subject to surveillance. In addition, ACJs switch their media identity cards, which are not always valid, to present themselves as either 'formal' journalists or 'alternative' according to context.

They also use various methods for protecting the visuals they have recorded from the police and the assault of government agents.

> The policeman noticed that I was filming when he tried to intercept my professional friends ... After a brief chase he caught me and dragged me to the custody vehicle ... A woman activist that I know approached and in the scuffle I managed to give her my SD card. When I got out I took it back and shared the photos and a short video over my Twitter account by mentioning almost all the alternative media channels.

Another problem of ACJs, like other journalists, is the hostility that they face from the state and/or paramilitary powers because of the content of their news. A journalist who worked freelance for AM and also for a CJ collective noted that s/he was tracked both offline and online, harassed, and threatened because of a very sensitive news story that s/he had published:

> I became the target of the news subject's political circle. First, I received DMs (direct messages) in my Twitter account. They said they knew my house and could come at any minute ... Then they sent photos of the street where I live ... I got so scared ...

The journalist, who was both digitally and physically tracked and surveyed, was still in a state of trauma when we spoke. Nevertheless, s/he managed to digitally block the tracking and used 'masking moves' to avoid being followed in the street (Marx, 2016). Furthermore, s/he stated that s/he might also have exposed the threat by confronting with a video camera the people who had threatened her/him and could have asked for help from solidarity networks after sharing this content. But s/he said that this was unnecessary because the threats ended a few days late.

All activist correspondents who acted as journalists during protests are also victims of assaults by the police, who purposely target them, even on occasions pointing a gun at them. Almost all correspondents note that the police knew them very well, and whenever they found the chance, had attacked them with tear gas, rubber bullets, or as individuals. Almost all of the correspondents assert that these attacks are all recorded and it is hoped that these witness videos of brutal attacks will one day make their way into a courtroom. It is not easy to remain safe even though real and/or virtual precautionary measures are taken, such as using digital security tools, disguises, and sousveillance (Marx, 2016; Mann et al., 2003).

In the responses to questions about ensuring the safety of individuals and news subjects, most of the ACJs note that they were cautious about hiding anyone mentioned in the news. The news subjects carry out their filming in a manner that takes no risks and protects the news subjects from getting caught by the state when these individuals are enacting what is termed criminal. Because of the risk that the images captured by ACJs might become surveillance tools of the state, the practical ethic of the CJs is primarily to protect the news subjects, and prevent them from being identified by the state. New tracking software such as face recognition added to the capabilities of CCTV cameras has made it easier for demonstrators to be recognized through their clothes, accessories, birthmarks, tattoos, etc. (Monahan, 2015). In this respect, ACJs use their cameras according to the demands of the demonstrators and also carefully try to ensure the safety of videos and photographs that might be seized in the production of news items. In addition to the safety of the news subject and the journalist, it is vital to avoid state surveillance by being wary that one may be used unwillingly and unknowingly as part of a panoptic trap (de Souza, 2014, p. 226).

The interview data provide concrete evidence that phones have been wiretapped to back up the accusations filed against journalists. It is also suspected that the police have sometimes successfully tried to infiltrate journalists' online communication channels (e-mail, etc.) and applications (WhatsApp, etc.). Therefore, news collective staff note that they take extra precautions when they use their phones, e-mails, or a chatting application. They strive to avoid producing content that may be deemed criminal. But they also note that when they try to produce news from places where and with people who are not welcomed by the state, they are subject to surveillance, harassment, or attack by the police and/or the military. The news that they report is usually added to their official files as a terrorist propaganda and is considered illegal.

According to our data, digital security is a crucial defence practice against state surveillance. However, it seems that awareness, technical knowledge, and practices are insufficient, despite the well-intentioned efforts of activists. In fact, ACJs are amateurs when it comes to protecting themselves against digital surveillance. They use conventional stashing methods in order to hide their archives or delete visuals that may cause legal problems. They format their hard disks in order to prevent their archives from being seized. We observed that news collectives have a better understanding of digital security and offer training sessions on this subject to the ACJs who have collaborated with them. Despite the training they receive, ACJs are reluctant to use digital security measures unless they are compelled by the collectives they are working with.

> We know that we are constantly followed online and our phones are wiretapped … And we even think that they do remote listening from time to time. So, all our communications are carried carefully. But using digital security tools is not always practical … time-consuming. Besides, we don't much like to give the impression that we are doing something illegal.

Yet almost all the ACJs whom we interviewed noted that they were careful about ensuring the security of both news subjects and sources. They stated that they also made mistakes that caused unwanted results. They are especially aware that the photographs or videos that they take in the heat of the moment or streaming live via social media may carry risk. However, they have few clear ideas about taking precautions, and they admit that even though the training creates awareness; they still have shortcomings in the area of skills.

Concluding remarks

Concerns are rising about democracy's vulnerability to ubiquitous state surveillance by authoritarian regimes, including Turkey's. At present, business relations, commercial risks, and enormous political pressure compel the national mainstream media to be pro-government and partisan. Thus, most of the professional and independent journalism that holds power accountable has disappeared. Many investigative journalists are still imprisoned; others have already gone abroad to be able to do their job more freely. Meantime, under the gaze of the state, the country's critical journalism is withering.

Given the analysis and discussion, in a study of this kind it is worth mentioning that the representatives (organizations and individuals) of the ANM, which we believe are nodal points within and between NSMs, have crucial potential through their informational, communicational, and collaborative roles in expanding or maintaining pro-democratic social movements. Therefore, we stress the need to combine theories about AM, social movements, and surveillance, making an interdisciplinary framework to advance our understanding. Within this framework, we focused on the counter-surveillance imaginaries and tactics of ACJs, working individually or in collectives.

We collected data through in-depth interviews with 22 activists. The advantages of in-depth interviews are many. First, this method of data collection simplifies and manages data without destroying complexity and content. Second, they give greater freedom to the interviewer to explore complex issues. Moreover, interviewing allows respondents to describe their experiences and interpretations vividly in comfortable conditions. As a result, their evidence suggests that critical news-making, including journalistic sousveillance in itself, could be considered an offensive move; defensive tactics more closely concern security for people at risk and protecting journalistic work in all forms and phases against state surveillance.

Finally, the study's limitations should be admitted. First, it has been difficult to paint a picture conveying all the relevant information when anonymity and safety are at stake. A few anonymous ACJs could not be contacted. Building confidence among our respondents and trust in our discretion was not only difficult but also hazardous for both sides. Thus, we sometimes felt that activists hesitated to reveal valuable data. For instance, the ACJs, particularly those working with collectives, were reluctant to answer questions about hacking and leaking practices. Second, although more than half of the respondents' journalistic routines involve no office work, in-depth interviews are insufficient to learn about the speakers' daily routines in more detail. In this regard, participant observation would have been a more appropriate method. Third, not being funded by any scientific institution in Turkey, we had to limit our selection to activists from İstanbul, leading to an incomplete data set. All these shortcomings should be addressed in future studies.

Disclosure statement

No potential conflict of interest was reported by the authors.

Notes on contributors

Dr. Bora Ataman is an Associate Professor of Communication Sciences at Arts & Sciences Faculty, Dogus University. He is currently studying on topics such as activist citizen journalism, media activism and counter-surveillance, and journalism safety. Recent co-authored research articles include; 'The Gezi Resistance and Activist Citizen Reporters' published by De Gruyter's Communications journal in Vol. 42, issue 1, in March 2017 and 'How safe is it? Being an Activist Citizen Journalist in Turkey' published in an edited book titled 'The Assault on Journalism' (Carlsson & Pöyhtari, 2017) by Nordicom.

Barış Çoban is Professor of Communication Sciences at Doğuş University, Turkey. His research interests are alternative media, new social movements and surveillance studies.

References

Allan, S. (2009). Histories of citizen journalism. In E. Thorsen, & S. Allan (Eds.), *Citizen journalism* (Vol. 1, pp. 17–31). New York, NY: Peter Lang.

Andrejevic, M. (2017). Digital citizenship and surveillance. *International Journal of Communication, 11*, 879–896.
Ataman, B., & Çoban, B. (2016). Alternatif medya ve anti-gözetim. In B. Çoban, & B. Ataman (Eds.), *Panoptikon* (pp. 33–47). İstanbul: EMO Yayın.
Atkinson, J. D. (2010). *Alternative media and politics of resistance*. New York, NY: Peter Lang.
Atton, C. (2002). News cultures and new social movements: Radical journalism and the mainstream media. *Journalism Studies, 3*(4), 491–505.
Atton, C., & Hamilton, J. F. (2008). *Alternative journalism*. London: Sage.
BİA. (2014, February 19). *Dava uyuyan hakimle devam edecek*. Retrieved from https://m.bianet.org/bianet/insan-haklari/153607-dava-uyuyan-hakimle-devam-edecek
Baran, S. J., & Davis, D. K. (2012). *Mass communication theory*. Boston, MA: Wadsworth.
Bauman, Z., Bigo, D., Esteves, P., Guild, E., Jabri, V., Lyon, D., & Walker, R. B. J. (2014). After snowden: Rethinking the impact of surveillance. *International Political Sociology, 8*, 121–144.
Bennett, L. (2017). Who are the people? Communication, power, and the rise of anti-democratic politics. In *ORF, TEXTE* (pp. 4–23). Wien: ORF-Druckerei.
Bennett, W. L., & Segerberg, A. (2013). *The logic of connective action. Digital media and the personalization of contentious politics*. New York, NY: Cambridge University Press.
Boykoff, J. (2006). *The suppression of dissent*. New York, NY: Routledge.
Brennen, B. S. (2013). *Qualitative research methods for media studies*. London: Routledge.
Carlsson, U., & Pöyhtäri, R. (2017). Words of introduction. In U. Carlsson, & R. Pöyhtäri (Eds.), *The assault on journalism* (pp. 11–17). Göteborg: Nordicom.
Castells, M. (2012). *Networks of outrage and hope*. Cambridge: Polity.
Çoban, B., & Ataman, B. (2017). The Gezi resistance and activist citizen reporters. *Communications, 42*(1), 1–22.
Committee to Protect Journalists (CPJ). *Turkey crackdown chronicle*. Retrieved from https://cpj.org
Davenport, C., Johnston, H., & Mueller, H. (Eds.). 2005. *Repression and mobilization*. Minneapolis, MN: University of Minnesota Press.
Dencik, L., & Cable, J. (2017). The advent of surveillance realism. *International Journal of Communication, 11*, 763–781.
Dencik, L., & Wilkin, P. (2015). *Worker resistance and the media*. Oxford: Peter Lang.
de Souza, R. M. (2014). Inverse surveillance, activist journalism and the Brazilian protests: The midia NINJA case. *Birkbeck Law Review, 2*, 211–227.
Deuze, M. (2005). What is journalism? *Journalism, 6*(4), 442–464.
Diken. (2017, October 12). *Red Hack Davası Öncesi Çağrı*. Retrieved from http://www.diken.com.tr/redhack-davasi-oncesi-cagri-gazetecilik-bu-degilse-ne/
Doğu, B. (2017). Turkey's news media landscape in Twitter: Mapping interconnections among diversity. *Journalism: Theory, Practice & Criticism*. doi:10.1177/1464884917713791
Downing, J., Ford, T., Gil, G., & Stein, L. (2001). *Radical media: Rebellious communication and social movements*. Thousand Oaks, CA: Sage.
The EIU. (2017). *Democracy index* 2017. A report by the Economist intelligence unit.
Fernandez, L., & Huey, L. (2009). Is resistance futile? Thoughts on resisting surveillance. *Surveillance & Society, Surveillance and Resistance Issue, 6*(3), 199–202.
Foucault, M. (1977). *Discipline and punish: The birth of the prison*. New York, NY: Random House.
Freedom House. (2013). *Democracy in crisis: Corruption, media and power in Turkey*. Retrieved from https://freedomhouse.org/sites/default/files/Turkey%20Report%20-%202-3-14.pdf
Freedom House. (2017a). *Freedom in the world. Populists and autocrats: The dual threat to global democracy*. Retrieved from https://freedomhouse.org/sites/default/files/FH_FIW_2017_Report_Final.pdf
Freedom House. (2017b). *Freedom of the press 2017: Turkey*. Retrieved from https://freedomhouse.org/report/freedom-press/2017/turkey
Freedom House/FOTN. (2017). Turkey. Retrieved from https://freedomhouse.org/sites/default/files/FOTN%202017_Turkey.pdf.
Ganascia, J. G. (2010). The generalized sousveillance society. *Social Science Information, 49*(3), 489–507.

Gaskell, G. (2000). Individual and group interviewing. In M. W. Bauer, & G. Gaskell (Eds.), *Qualitative researching with text, image and sound* (pp. 38–56). London: Sage.
Gerbaudo, P. (2012). *Tweets and streets*. London: Pluto.
Harcourt, B. E. (2013). Political disobedience. In W. J. T. Mitchell, B. E. Harcourt, & M. Taussig (Eds.), *Occupy*, (pp. 45–91). Chicago, IL: The University of Chicago Press.
Harvey, D. (2014). *Seventeen contradictions and the end of capitalism*. Oxford: Oxford University Press.
Held, D. (1987). *Models of democracy*. Cambridge: Polity Press.
Hem, M. (2014). *Evading the censors: Critical journalism in authoritarian states*. Oxford: University of Oxford. Reuters Institute for the Study of Journalism.
Henrichsen, J., Betz, M., & Lisosky, J. (2015). *Building digital safety for journalism*. Paris: UNESCO.
Hermida, A., & Hernández-Santaolalla, V. (2017). Twitter and video activism as tools for counter-surveillance. *Information, Communication & Society*. doi:10.1080/1369118X.2017.1284880
Hintz, A., Dencik, L., & Wahl-Jorgensen, K. (2017). Digital citizenship and surveillance. *International Journal of Communication, 11*, 731–739.
Hobsbawm, E. (2007). *Globalisation, democracy and terrorism*. London: Abacus.
Human Rights Watch. (2016). *Silencing Turkey's media*. Retrieved from https://www.hrw.org/report/2016/12/15/silencing-turkeys-media/governments-deepening-assault-critical-journalism
Isın, E., & Ruppert, E. (2015). *Being digital citizens*. London: Rowman & Littlefield.
Juris, J. S. (2004). Networked social movements. In M. Castells (Ed.), *The network society* (pp. 341–362). Cheltenham: Edward Elgar.
Juris, J. S. (2005). The new digital media and activist networking within anti–corporate globalization movements. *The ANNALS of the American Academy of Political and Social Science, 597*(1), 189–208.
Juris, J. S., & Khasnabish, A. (Eds.). 2013. *Insurgent encounters: Transnational activism, ethnography, and the political*. Durham: Duke University Press.
Kurban, D., & Sözeri, C. (2012). *İktidarın çarkında medya*. İstanbul: TESEV.
Langman, L. (2005). From virtual public spheres to global justice: A critical theory of internetworked social movements. *Sociological Theory, 23*(1), 42–74.
Leistert, O. (2012). Resistance against cyber-surveillance within social movements and how surveillance adapts. *Surveillance & Society, 9*(4), 441–456.
Lievrouw, L. A. (2011). *Alternative and activist new media*. Cambridge: Polity Press.
Lyon, D. (1994). *The electronic eye*. Cambridge: Polity Press.
Lyon, D. (2001). *Surveillance society: Monitoring everyday life*. Oxford: Open University Press.
Lyon, D. (2017). Surveillance culture. *International Journal of Communication, 11*, 824–842.
Mann, S., Nolan, J., & Wellman, B. (2003). Sousveillance. *Surveillance & Society, 1*(3), 331–355.
Marx, G. T. (2016). *Windows into the soul*. Chicago, IL: University of Chicago Press.
McChesney, R. W., & Nichols, J. (2016). *People get ready: The fight against a jobless economy and a citizenless democracy*. New York, NY: Nation Books.
Mills, A., & Sarikakis, K. (2016). Reluctant activists? *Big Data & Society, 3*(2), 1–11.
Monahan, T. (2006). Counter-surveillance as political intervention? *Social Semiotics, 16*(4), 515–534.
Monahan, T. (2015). The right to hide? Anti-surveillance camouflage and the aestheticization of resistance. *Communication and Critical/Cultural Studies, 12*(2), 159–178.
Murakami Wood, D. (2017). Editorial: The global turn to authoritarianism and after. *Surveillance & Society, 15*(3/4), 357–370.
Nayar, P. K. (2015). *Citizenship and identity in the age of surveillance*. Cambridge: Cambridge University Press.
Orwell, G. (1949). *Nineteen eighty-four*. New York, IL: Harcourt, Brace.
Özel, Y., & Uyanık, Ş. (2016). "Karakutu" Bir Bilgi Sızdırma Platformu. In B. Çoban, & B. Ataman (Eds.), *Panoptikon* (pp. 71–75). İstanbul: EMO.
Radsch, C. (2011). Arab bloggers as citizen journalists. In J. Downing (Ed.), *Encyclopaedia of social movement media* (pp. 61–64). Thousand Oaks, CA: Sage.

Rice, R. (2017). Resisting NSA data collection through media-activism and public sousveillance. In B. Çoban, & B. Ataman (Eds.), *Panoptikon 2.0* (pp. 205–224). İstanbul: Kafka.
Rosen, J. (2006). The People formerly known as the audience. *Pressthink*. Retrieved from http://archive.pressthink.org/2006/06/27/ppl_frmr.html
RSF Press Freedom Index. (2017). Turkey. Retrieved from https://rsf.org/en/turkey.
Sambrook, R. (2016). Reporting in uncivil societies and why it matters. In S. Cottle, R. Sambrook, & N. Mosdell (Eds.), *Reporting dangerously* (pp. 17–35). London: Palgrave Macmillan.
Shaw, F. (2013). 'Walls of seeing': Protest surveillance, embodied boundaries, and counter-surveillance at occupy Sydney. *Transformations: Journal of Media & Culture, 23*, 1–9.
TGS. (2018, January 26). *151 Gazeteci ve Medya Çalışanı Cezaevinde*. https://tgs.org.tr/cezaevindeki-gazeteciler/
Topak, E. (2017). The making of a totalitarian surveillance machine: Surveillance in Turkey under AKP rule. *Surveillance & Society, 15*(3/4), 535–542.
Tuğal, C. (2013). "Resistance everywhere": The gezi revolt in global perspective. *New Perspectives on Turkey, 49*, 157–172.
Tükekçi, Z. (2017). *Twitter and tear gas: The power and fragility of networked protest*. New Haven: Yale University Press.
Van Dijk, J. (2012). *The network society*. London: Sage.
Waghorn, N. J. (2016). Watching the watchmen: Resisting drones and the 'protester panopticon'. *Geographica Helvetica, 71*(2), 99–108.
Wahl-Jorgensen, K., Hintz, A., Dencik, L., & Bennett, L. (2017). Introduction: Journalism, citizenship and surveillance. *Digital Journalism, 5*(3), 256–261.
Wilson, D. (2012). Counter-surveillance, protest and policing. *Plymouth Law and Criminal Justice Review, 4*, 33–42.
Wilson, D., & Serisier, T. (2010). Video activism and the ambiguities of counter-surveillance. *Surveillance and Society, 8*(2), 166–180.
WJP. (2018). *Rule of law index 2017*–2018. Retrieved from https://worldjusticeproject.org/sites/default/files/documents/WJP_ROLI_2017-18_Online-Edition.pdf
Yeşil, B., & Sözeri, E. K. (2017). Online surveillance in Turkey. *Surveillance & Society, 15*(3/4), 543–549.
Zizek, S. (2012). *The year of dreaming dangerously*. London: Verso.
Zuboff, S. (2016). *The secrets of surveillance capitalism*. Retrieved from http://www.faz.net/aktuell/feuilleton/debatten/the-digital-debate/shoshana-zuboff-secrets-ofsurveillance-capitalism-14103616.html?printPagedArticle=true#pageIndex_2

Index